TO THE TOP

SIMPLE EVERYDAY STEPS TO SUCCEED FINANCIALLY

BY ERIC TIPPETTS

Copyright

TO THE TOP Copyright © 2014 by Rockstar Products, LLC

First Published: December 2014

Published by: Rockstar Products
32565 B. Golden Lantern #222 Dana Point, CA 92629

ISBN: 978-0-9903239-0-7

For more information, visit www.erictippetts.com
or send all inquiries and orders to info@erictippetts.com

Table of Contents

Preface

Twenty-two years ago my wife and I lived in a studio apartment just big enough for a queen-size bed and our stereo equipment—in Southern California. I was struggling to pay rent, our car payment/insurance and food. I was naive to wealth and didn't understand anything about finances, from making money to managing it. I was trying to become a professional actor/model and leave my mark on the world. One year later (after a New Year's celebration, naturally) we decided that we were going to stop being "OK" with barely making it and instead set our intention to becoming better…in every area of our lives.

We devoted our television time to reading books together. Instead of eating out, we made dinner for one another. Instead of being scared, we encouraged each other to take leaps of faith. We pushed each other out of comfort and into a reality of growth/change/enlightenment passion and, best of all, abundance!

That year after taking action towards our goals, I booked the worldwide Levi's campaign for both TV and print (billboards, retail stores, etc.). We went from scraping by to tens of thousands of dollars coming in faster than we could spend it. I thought it would never end. We had finally made it! We were rich!!

Within one year, we went from being "rich" to wondering where all the money had gone. What had we done?! How could this happen? Where did we go wrong?

What I realized is that I stopped doing the very things that had created this wealth. I stopped growing. I had become comfortable.

In the last twenty years I have made millions and lost millions, and what I have realized is that life is truly a journey of lessons. Take pleasure in learning the ups and downs. Take chances or you will always look back and wonder, "What if?" Fear is the thief of dreams; don't let it steal yours!

I wrote this book to help you not make the same mistakes I did and also to encourage you to take action to build your dreams.

Don't waste one day! It might be your last. You have a choice every day you wake up—it's either going to be a bad day or an AMAZING ONE! Choose amazing!

Never stop learning and growing. That was the biggest mistake I made in the year I lost it all; I had simply stopped.

Remember too that "leaders are readers." Commit to reading 30 minutes per day on topics you want to learn. You'll be amazed at the excitement and joy it will bring into your life.

Lastly, the key to financial success: building wealth starts with your mindset. You attract what you think about most. Do you have a mindset of abundance or poverty? Do you feel wealthy or do you feel poor? Your mind will always guide your actions. Start each day by setting your intentions on what you want. Be as specific as possible on every detail to create this reality in your mind. Then take action like you have this goal already.

You create your own reality!

I believe in you! Probably more than you believe in yourself. Each one of us has gifts…Find yours and enjoy them!

So much love,

Credits

Cover Image Designer: Brian Tippetts
Layout & Illustration Designer: Bonnevie Ycot Pepito
Proofreader: Lauren Vanessa Zink

Acknowledgement

I am blessed to be surrounded by incredible people that always empower me to evolve every day. I would like to thank two special people in helping fulfill my dream to become an author so I can contribute to the world.

Beth Tippetts and Dr. Robert Tippetts ("Mom" and "Dad"). Thank you for always believing in me and helping me dream big. I cherish my childhood and the lessons you both taught me. I strive every day to help my daughter experience these same experiences you gave me of a life full of hope, love, and laughter. Thank you.

This book is dedicated to my wife, Shelly and my daughter, Asia. You both are my foundation of life. Thank you for your love and support. I love you both more and more every day!

Love,

Your Husband and Dad

Testimonials

"Eric speaks straight truth every person looking to create more wealth needs to hear. There are numerable ways an average person can retain and make more money reading this book. Awesome work Eric!"

-Jonathan Budd

"An amazing read for anyone wanting to move up the financial ladder! More importantly, this book teaches you exactly how to grab full control of your economic situation…and improve it now!"

-Todd Falcone, Sales Trainer and Personal Development Coach

"I think your book is very well done and speaks to the reader in a professional yet easy-to-understand-and-implement format. It will be a great on-line reference guide for any person who is ready to take action for self-improvement and not afraid to risk putting themselves in a position to be successful. Congratulations!!"

-Joel Ray, CEO, New Benefits

"Eric's book is a must read for anyone and everyone who is wanting to become financially free. He has put not only the strategies for creating wealth, but he has eloquently dealt with the mental and emotional issues that so often hold people back from doing what they know needs to be done. Congratulations Eric, you have a winner here and I'm sure you'll inspire people across the planet to create wealth."

-Jim Bunch, CEO, The Ultimate Game of Life

I. Keep Your Finances Under Control to Live a Better Life

A mortgage to buy a nice house, a car or two, a secure job that delivers a bi-weekly paycheck, the luxury of health insurance, and of course, a nice family to share it all with. Many middle-class Americans live this American dream without thinking about the implications, without knowing what it really means.

Do you live the fragile American dream, too?

Most Americans do not realize just how fragile the American dream is, that their lives might be shattered in under a minute. Have you ever considered what would happen if you experienced one of the following?

- A financial crisis, like the 2008 Lehman Brothers collapse, that you are not prepared for?

- A government shutdown that leaves you without your habitual paycheck or annuity?

- An unexpected expense that you cannot cover without taking out an expensive loan?
- The loss of a job by either husband or wife or both?
- An unfortunate accident that leaves you crippled and unable to provide for your family?
- Or worse, an accident or a sickness that takes you away from your family, bequeathing them not only pain and grief, but also debt, bills, uncertainty?

Maybe you think that these things cannot happen to someone like you, but I assure you that they can and frequently do. The past five years and their continuing economic uncertainty have proven that we are all exposed to these dangers. You are exceptional, but you are no exception!

And sadly, in many cases, should something unexpected happen, you are not only out of the workforce, but most probably out of the American dream, too.

Unless... unless....

This book is about everything that might be written after "unless." This book will not tell you how to avert an economic crisis, an unexpected layoff, a debilitating sickness or death, but it will most certainly tell you how to be prepared for these unexpected and sad occasions. It will tell you how to protect yourself and your loved ones from the aftermath as much as possible. In this sense, you can and you should be the exception by being prepared.

Are you 'naked' to the world?

The first and most important thing is that you have to understand that debt (and any other kind of unnecessary exposure to financial weaknesses) is in most cases dangerous for your family. I am not talking about the loan that your business (if you have one) took out in order to be able to innovate, though I do hope that you have found a legal way to ensure that your limited liability will indeed remain limited in case of problems, too. I am talking about mortgages, consumer loans, credit card debts and any other type of private debt; most Americans use all of these financial instruments without knowing just how dangerous they are. Most Americans use these financial instruments without knowing that they keep users in servitude.

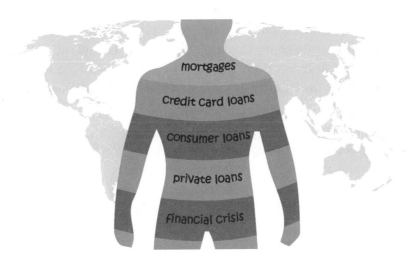

Yes, you've read that right. When you are in debt, you are not a free person. You are not free to handle your finances the way you want to or need to. When you are in debt, your debtor handles an important chunk of your income, and the worst part of this is the fact that these debts are often long-term debts that might cripple your family for years, sometimes even for decades. When you are in debt, you are naked to the world. This means that you can be even more hurt by those famous external and unexpected factors like financial crises, economic downturns, and company bankruptcy. It is like going out without your clothes on, with nothing protecting you against the winter cold.

Are you a victim, too?

Many people who live the fragile American dream are ruined when (to continue the metaphor) the cold comes and catches them naked.

Many people, ruined by the unexpected, often pose as innocent victims. They consider themselves victims of the system, of the government, of Wall Street, of the WTO, of their employer, their parentage, or, in worse cases where they are receptive to racism, they consider themselves victims of immigration, of Mexicans, of Jews--you name it; the list goes on.

But you, who dreams of financial stability and security, who dreams of independence and freedom, who wants to live the American dream in relative security, you should know better than that. Luckily, since you have decided to read a book like this, I can safely assume that you already know **that the quality of your financial future depends on you and you alone.**

So all those people who blame their problems on everybody but themselves, they are victims, all right, but they are perpetrators as well Their unconsciousness or ignorance is a crime: negligence. They are the people who neglected to lan their financial future. They are the people who did not examine their weaknesses and made no steps to cut them out. They are the people who founded a family on a single income and forgot to take out a life insurance policy to secure the future of that family should anything happen to the provider...

But since you are here, since you are about to read this book, you know that you have responsibilities to yourself, your family and your loved ones. You know that we live in fragile and insecure times (a cliché, but true). However, you also know that you can master your future, that there is no reason why you should continue to be a victim. You are sitting here reading this book because you are ready to take your life back and because you want answers. You want to know how to be an independent and financially free person.

This book will give you the answers you are looking for. I am not telling you that this book will give you all the answers; however, I will tell you where to look for more information, should the need arise.

By the end of this book, you will be able to:

- Analyze and assess your personal financial situation.
- Identify the weak points in your finances.
- Bring order into your books.
- Get out of debt as soon as possible.
- Control your personal spending and your taxes.
- Prepare a living will, advance directives, and trusts.
- Use life insurance effectively and understand the reasons for life insurance policies.
- Protect your identity from being stolen and understand the basic methods of self defense.
- Create a "gold reserve," an emergency reserve of food and cash ready for you should your family find itself without income
- Finally, at the end of the book, use capital and value creation, investments, and asset allocation to your advantage.

To sum up this long list, this book will guide you through three very logical steps:

1. **Making order in your books and getting out of debt**
2. **Preparing for the future in terms of self defense**
3. **Creating capital and wealth**

I know that it might seem a lot to learn. It might even be overwhelming at first. But you will see that controlling one's finances is not that hard; in fact, throughout this book, I will walk you through a very logical path towards financial stability and security. You only have to come with me and learn what you have to learn and do what you have to do.

It depends on you.

As I am writing these lines (October 2013), the U.S. government is shut down, and, if parties fail to reach a reasonable budget agreement as soon as possible, we are only a few days away from an unprecedented national credit default. Many Americans find themselves under a cloud now. For instance, those who work for or depend on the government did not receive their paychecks or their annuities because the federal shop is closed. If they have no gold reserve, if they have no emergency food and cash put aside, they are in a real mess now! See, they are naked or vulnerable to the affairs of the world, and they are even exposed to such seemingly far away and mundane things as party politics!

If you are not one among them, say a little prayer and prepare for other dangers that might threaten you. If you are one of them, come along with me and learn to be your own master. Learn to be prepared.

Controlling our finances has never been more important. There is no magic formula; controlling your finances means working on your finances. Finances need consistent, regular work and regular attention; this is the real hardship of finances--not difficulty or complexity!

Only you can help yourself. Only you can control your finances and frankly, you should. (You are here, so you already know this!) Do not wait for others; neither your mother nor the government will help you if you do not help yourself.

Take the control back now. Control your life and your finances to attain liberty, to have a better life.

A better life? Yes, exactly. Those who are financially secure need not worry nor be anxious about tomorrow. They can live for today. They can sleep tranquilly, knowing that they have done everything they could in order to protect themselves and their families from the unexpected. Or simply put, they are less anxious about the future, about politics, and about their job, so they have more strength and more quality time to spend with their loved ones. This wonderful sense of security and control also raises their self-esteem. These are the people who know who they are, know what they are worth, and emit a

I. Keep Your Finances Under Control to Live a Better Life

peaceful sense of joy.

When you attain this phase (preferably by the end of the book), you will also realize that financial security is on your inside, not on your outside. Financial security and wealth is not about appearances and about the latest car model; richness is not always visible. Many rich people hide their wealth, not because they are ashamed of it but because they have a sufficiently strong self-esteem and do not need to brag about what they have.

Dear Friend,

Are you ready for this journey? Are you ready to walk the path with me towards your financial stability and security? Are you ready to take back the control and to live the financially secure, strong American dream, the life that you have always dreamt of? If your answer is yes and I know it is, since you are here, be prepared for a huge change!

This book will change your life for the better, but only if you work with us. Remember? There is no magic formula. Controlling your finances means regularly and consistently working on your finances.

I advise you not to run through this book hurriedly. I ask you to read it chapter by chapter. Please think about the things that you read and try to do all the exercises, all the steps. Do not skip chapters, do not skip steps, do not skip exercises. Not because I insist on them, but because one step logically comes from the other. If you do not make order in your books, you will not be able to prepare your family for the future and will not be able to create wealth and capital. Similarly, there is no sense in investing if you have no emergency cash and food set aside.

I wish you fun while reading, and I really hope that our common journey will result in something really big, something really good: **a new YOU, a financially secure person who is ready to enjoy and live life without anxiety and fear!**

Let's get going!

Most sincerely,

II. Understand the Law of Life - Choose Your Attitude, Commitment, and Momentum

"I am not rich. I am a poor man with money, which is not the same thing. - Gabriel García Marquez

The key to being happy with money is our attitude about the "riches" of life. It is okay to desire the 'blessings" of basic prosperity and financial security—*if you are willing to work hard for them by doing a few basic things!*

This book is about cause and effect, actions and consequences. When you want something positive (an effect or result), you have to do something positive (a cause or action). Our actions (or inactions) have consequences. You can trust that this basic law of life will work for you in your quest for financial security and prosperity. You can be happy and "rich" in your life, whatever that might mean to you, by taking positive action now.

When we choose to take control of our finances and to prepare for prosperity, when we exercise our will, we set in motion forces and momentum that lead to results or consequences.

That is a law of life: cause and effect, actions and consequences.

If you want something, when you will it to be so, when you set the forces in motion to get it for you and persist in working those forces, the consequences are certain. If you want something, but do not will it sufficiently enough to work hard to get it, then, of course, nothing will happen.

We all know how the law of cause and effect, of actions and consequences, works.

This book is about what some call 'tough love;' actions have consequences. We can choose our attitude towards wealth and prosperity, we can choose to make the commitments to bring about our prosperity goals, and we can choose to put into motion sufficient actions to reap the consequences or effects of those choices. That is a law of life and a wonderful law of hope in our lives.

The only person in your personal life who can define your financial goals and purpose is you. That means taking ownership for the results in your life and stopping making excuses and blaming others for the condition of your life. Your life is exactly the way it is because of the actions you have taken—actions have predictable consequences. If you don't like the way your life has turned out, you have the power to change. Again, actions have consequences.

We know this law works. You can do it, if you will it and work hard to get it! First, get your attitude right for the task. Second, make the commitment to do what is required. And third, seek the momentum that can push or surge energy into your work to ensure you reach your goal.

Once those forces are in place, then you can put into place the plans and documents to bring about the degree of prosperity and financial security you want in your life.

In this book I will walk you through a proven process that will lead you to success with your financial goals. At the conclusion of the book, you will see this table, which asks you to log in your accomplishment of each of the seven tasks for prosperity and financial security:

I CAN DO IT	DATE ACCOMPLISHED	DATE
Attitude/Commitment/ Momentum		
Analyze your Situation		
Budget		
Home-Based Business		
Control your Spending		
Retirement Plan		
Will		
Living Trust		
Life Insurance		
Emergency Cash and Food		
Identity Theft		

Okay, let's get to work!

Attitude

"I am positive that personal finance is 80 percent behavior and only 20 percent head knowledge.... To change your money you have to change you. You have to change your life.... The principles are not mine. I stole them from God and your grandmother. The principles are common sense...." (Ramsey, The Total Money Makeover, ix-x)

We have to believe firmly and positively that we can make changes and reach a goal of prosperity and financial security. We have to believe enough to will change in our lives. It is that choice, fundamentally, that determines all that will or can follow. In that choice is the action, the cause that is sufficient to set in motion the forces that will lead, inevitably, to the effects or consequences.

First of all, to engage you in thinking about the need for attitude, I desire to make a point about how significant attitude is in the minds of the major financial gurus who have published "self-help" books

Following is a semi-random, somewhat guided selection of personal finance-oriented "how-to" books (now alphabetized) from the 10 shelves (two racks) of about 200 books at a local Barnes & Noble Bookstore. Glance through the titles and think of what they are asking you to do, what the overriding theme seems to be:

- 7 Money Rules for Life: How to Take Control of Your Financial Future (Hunt 2012)
- Bitches on a Budget: Sage Advice for Surviving Tough Times in Style (Hoffman 2010)
- Create the Life You Really Want (Willis/Garn, 2011)
- Debt-Free Forever: Take Control of Your Money and Your life (Vaz-0xlade 2009)
- Easy Ways to Lower Your Taxes (USA Today, Block/Fishman 2008)
- Every Landlord's Tax Deduction Guide (Fishman 2010)
- Insurance for Dummies (Hungelmann 2009)
- Investing in an Uncertain Economy for Dummies (Garrett 2008)
- Managing Your Money All-in-One for Dummies (2009)
- Market Mind Games: A Radical Psychology of Investing, Trading and Risk (Skull 2012)
- Pay It Down: Debt-Free on $10 a Day (Chatzky 2009)
- Personal Finance for Dummies (Tyson 2010)
- The 10 Commandments of Money: Survive and Thrive in the New Economy (Weston 2011)
- The One-Minute Millionaire: The Enlightened Way to Wealth (Hansen/Allen 2009)
- The Psychology of Wealth: Understand Your Relationship with Money and Achieve Prosperity (Richard 2012)

- The Road to Wealth: the Answers You Need to More Than 2,000 Personal Finance Questions (Orman, 2010)
- The Smartest Money Book You'll Ever Read: Everything You Need to Know about Growing, Spending, and Enjoying Your Money (Solin 2012)
- The Total Money Makeover: A Proven Plan for Financial Fitness (Ramsey 2009)
- Your Money or Your Life (Robin/Dominguez/Tilford 2008)
- Your Money: The Missing Manual (Roth, 2010)
- You're Broke Because You Want To Be (Winget 2008)

In fact, when I glance through the Introductions of all of these books, what becomes clear quickly is:

THE MIND GAME OF CHOOSING OR DECIDING TO DO SOMETHING IS 99% OF THE STRUGGLE WITH CONTROL OF YOUR FINANCES.

We're not paying attention; our psychology about money and finances is not helping us. Our present negative state of affairs exists because we are choosing it to be that way.

"If you're like most people, the lack of planning and budgeting is precisely the problem. It's boring. It's a hassle and time-consuming." (Solin, xii)

We do not want to choose, to decide, because we perceive it to be so hard. Our perception is the problem, not the financial realities! We don't choose to act, to do something!

With each of the financial gurus, personal choice, personal attitude, personal belief is the beginning of any change we might want to make.

We need to believe, to have hope, to put our whole hearts into the effort to obtain financial security and prosperity in our lives. This is the first step, to put doubt behind you and to choose a positive attitude that you can reach the goal. You can do it! You CAN enjoy basic financial security! YOU CAN!

Wherever we are now, whatever our circumstances, however negative and despairing things seem today, tough love reminds us that we have to take responsibility for our actions. We have to accept the reality that the circumstances or consequences we face in our lives today are those we have chosen, consciously or unconsciously; we may not like them, but we have chosen them nevertheless. So, **we need to take responsibility for the present outcomes in our lives without blaming anyone or just giving up.** Actions have consequences. We have to see clearly our present condition and know, without a doubt, that we have the will to change it.

Achieving any goal is difficult, but the process is always the same. If you want something, you better really want it or will it enough to work to bring it about. **The good news for a change activity is that actions have consequences—good actions bring about good consequences. That is the law of life!**

As we read many books on "attraction marketing," the "Laws of Attraction," and many more...one thing I do not agree with is that you can just focus your mind on what you want and magically it shows up. The key is focusing on what you want in life and then going to work towards receiving this in your life...the more time you spend on focusing and action, the more it puts in motion your receiving this result.

Action + Preparation = Momentum (what some call luck)

Just remember, what you focus and think about most in your daily routine is what you will attract in your life. That is why so many people attract negative results in their life. They are always worried about what COULD go wrong that they attract negative things to happen. How many times have you worried and hoped something would not happen and BAM, it then happens and you get angry and grumble, "why me?" This is because you attracted this negativity into your life, and subconsciously you already knew it was going to happen and thus created the reality of it.

When I talk about attitude, we have a choice every day we wake up…. Is it going to be a GREAT day or is it going to be a BAD day? We really do have the choice, and when we decide, our actions and the consequences will follow our mental choice.

Cause-Effect, Actions-Consequences

Remember, as the author of **Investing in an Uncertain Economy for Dummies** says early in his book,

"You are your biggest asset, thanks to your ability to earn money, and you need to protect and develop that asset…. Invest in yourself, know your financial situation, keep your emotions in check." (7-9)

YOU CAN DO IT!

If we choose, if we decide to make a change in the financial trajectory in our lives, we can do it. We have everything we need within ourselves. "We are the biggest asset," and when we decide on a positive direction for our financial lives, then that is exactly what begins to come about.

How do you eat an elephant? One bite at a time! How do you make your way to heaven? One good deed at a time. How do you have a good marriage, how do you develop great children, how do you learn a language, how do you do anything? One step at a time. Hope, faith, action—these are words that people use to describe the mental state of those who decide, who make the choice to believe and to think positively and then move forward.

Remember the lesson or moral of Aesop's fable of the Tortoise and the Hare:

"Slow and steady wins the race!"

Think about it. The moral of this fable makes good sense. Slow down, pay attention, think it through. You know how to do this. Now, concerning a change in your financial situation, you need to decide, "I am going to do this! Day in, day out, easy days and hard days, I am going to do this. I know that if I choose to cause good things to happen and believe, then if I dedicate and commit myself to the necessary hard work, I can trust that the effects will come. Actions do have consequences! I can believe that. I see that as an operative true principle in my life. I can trust that this law of life is so."

Commitment

"If you didn't want to be broke, you wouldn't be broke. It's as simple as that. What you say you want means nothing. When every action you make contradicts your words, your words don't mean a darn thing.... Aligning our intentions with our actions is something we all can learn to do better. It is the key to unlock your potential, get out of debt, and get ahead in life. It is something you can learn, but in exchange you have to give something up.... Stop being a victim! (Winget, 3)

Once we decide, then action is required to put that belief or attitude into practice. Attitude is thinking and words; now we need actions and behavior. We are not victims; we are capable of making the changes necessary to gain prosperity and financial security. Here we go!

Seeing the end from the beginning

Stand tall, as it were, as if you were a watchman on a tall tower, with eyes to see and ears to hear far off. Look out over the weeks and months to come to see the realization of your vision of the financial security and prosperity that you want to bring into your life. There, you can see it done! Imagine the task complete, achieved, and see the steps that you have taken to get there.

Say to yourself, "I can see what I need to do clearly, so all I have to do now is get busy to accomplish the specific tasks. I have done hard things in my life; I know I can do this for me and my family!"

Once you see the end and understand the steps of how to get there, then it is easy to make the commitment to get it done.

"I will write my plan. I will get out of debt. I will get my taxes under control. I will prepare a will and set up a trust. I will get life insurance. I will set aside money and food for emergencies. I will protect my financial resources from identity theft. I can do each of those things right now!"

Cause/Effect. Actions/Consequences. If you see what you need to do and understand exactly the steps/tasks you need to accomplish to get there, then you will find it easy to make the commitment to get it done. Now it will make sense; it is possible! You have to believe that what is asked of you right now is to just start. Do the first thing. One step at a time. Get it done. When you have the first done, great! Now do the second thing. When you have it done, do the third thing.

Just start. Slow and steady wins the race. Actions have consequences; they always do! Take the positive and proper action, and reap the positive and proper consequence.

One recommendation is to create a "vision board." This is a paper or poster you hang on your wall that reminds you daily of what your financial goals are or what results you want in your life. This also helps you start to take action and track your steps to achieving these goals. When you want something, you need to write it down. This gets the idea out of your head and onto paper for accountability and reminds you of the results you want. Then you need to put a specific date that you want to reach this goal/result by. This will give it a time in your mind that you need to work towards to complete and achieve this goal.

To just say "I want a million dollars" is not productive. Of course you want a million dollars, but consciously and unconsciously you do not believe it….you need to believe it and say it with conviction and write it down and by what date you are going to achieve milestones.

Goal = Million Dollars or $1,000,000.00

Milestones: Jan. 15 at 1 pm, I will have $1,000 in my bank account. I will work 5 extra hours per week = $100 per week = $400 extra per month.

What you are seeing in the example above is that I am telling myself what I want and by what date and how I am going to start, the specific steps, putting action towards my goal. Your turn. "I will do what to earn X amount more per month?"

You will be amazed at the doors that start to open when you put motion behind ideas/thoughts towards your goals.

Today is the day! Stop convincing yourself to put off your dreams and goals. Everyone in everything they do started somewhere…it's your time to start today!

Momentum

Momentum is like magic. All of a sudden, seemingly from nowhere, when we have a strong and positive attitude, when we see the end and understand the steps to get there, when we just take the first step and start—WHAM, the magic happens! Momentum and energy move into the task, and we are swept away in the enjoyment and excitement of doing the work.

This "magic" energy is always present when someone has chosen a path, has a positive and hopeful attitude, has committed to reaching a specific goal, and is applying maximum focus and energy to the work. If you want to achieve your goal of prosperity and financial security, you must believe that this "magic" will happen when you exert faith, put your head down, and go to work. This power of momentum will sweep you towards your desired outcome.

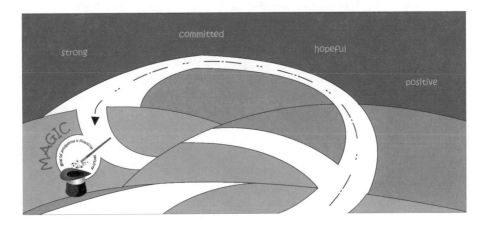

Action creates momentum, but the intensity of your actions determines the velocity for how fast you get there. Momentum is simply a by-product of your focused activity. When you focus, plan, and take action, you can activate this "magic" of momentum and achieve your desired goal.

If you focus your actions towards a specific result, you'll harness the momentum of your actions to bring that goal towards you at a much faster rate. When you have the positive momentum on your side, success and luck seem to come naturally as if you can do nothing wrong. A goal and a perfect plan, followed with disciplined action, will always guide your momentum towards your desired outcome. I know that is true because good and positive actions, backed up by a specific plan and genuine effort and hard work, **ALWAYS BRING ABOUT GOOD AND POSITIVE CONSEQUENCES.**

That is the law of life.

In this chapter, you learned:

- The importance attitude plays in your wealth money management.

- Every action you take has a consequence.

- Consistent, small actions are better than starting and stopping.

- Setting goals and milestones can inspire you when it gets challenging.

- Your movements will create momentum. So what are you waiting for?

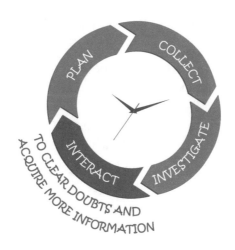

III. Intellectual Prototyping

"If a picture is worth a thousand words, then I think a prototype is worth a thousand ideas. Most ideas originate as a few words on a page, or a nascent concept in one person's head. Developing a physical prototype or representation of the idea will spawn new ideas and new insights. Yet few firms do anything to encourage rapid prototyping as a means to develop and refine ideas. Far too often teams generate ideas in brainstorming sessions, record ideas on a flipchart and fail to develop the ideas in any meaningful way. Prototyping—building very simple representations of ideas—will help people understand the ideas more effectively, will help teams understand the value proposition of an idea, and will help people interact and provide refinements and identify weaknesses. Individuals and teams who aren't creative can, in less than 30 minutes, significantly improve an idea and gain dramatically better insights." (Jeffrey Phillips, "Why Prototyping is integral to innovation," Innovate on Purpose, http://innovateonpurpose.blogspot.com/2011/11/why-prototyping-is-integral-to.html)

Prototypes are physical things to think with, to make thinking better. In this chapter I will show you how to do prototyping in support of your search for prosperity and financial security.

This is going to be a fun and liberating chapter for you as you begin your preparation for prosperity and financial security. It is the "enabler," the "thinking and researching tool" that you will use throughout the chapters of this book as you put into place the steps that we will discuss. Do you know how to "play around" with ideas, how to "mess around with something to try to understand it," to "goof off" with ideas with others as you collaborate to seek solutions and answers?

As you begin to consider each of the steps I will introduce to you, start by a process of flooding your mind (and notebook) with information, from here, there, everywhere. Go to the bookstore, go online, go to your neighbor or family, go to an expert or guru—loosen up. Forget being perfect or taking too much time. Just gather and play around with information for a while.

Here's an example of "looking around" to help with thinking:

When cowboys round up cattle in the fall of the year that have been ranging in a National Forest for about three months, they park the cattle hauling trucks down at the lowest meadow at the base of the mountains where the holding pens are located. Then, they start the cattle drive by riding their horses far out to the boundary of the forest land, as far out as an animal can go, and then they begin to ride around that furthest boundary in a circle, finding animals and pushing them downhill. When they find an animal, they don't chase it. They just start moving. Then they ride back out to the furthest boundary and keep going around, staying out, finding all the animals. When they have everything found and started down, then they start coming down towards the holding pens and trunks, in smaller and smaller circles, pushing animals down, knowing that they have all animals moving in the roundup.

Finally, they have all animals driven into the holding pens and loaded onto the trucks and the roundup is complete—all animals accounted for and the solution now complete.

This is exactly what you do when you first encounter one of the steps I will recommend to you in the following chapters. You begin a simple thinking and prototyping process of "finding the animals," all of them, finding all possible ideas, making sure you miss none of them, and then you keep pushing on them and riding them down and down, thinking about them, adding new stuff all of the time, until you come to see what you have, what it means, and how you can form a solution that fits your situation.

It is a very satisfying process because it is so personal and so practical.

But you know this process already—you do it when you go to buy a new car, when you want to buy a new home, when you are interested in a marriageable companion, etc. Sometimes formally, most of the time informally. You start a process of search and analysis that goes around and around until, finally, you know what is going on, you have all of the necessary information, you see a clear path, and you now see the decisions and actions you must take.

"We talk a lot about prototypes in innovation–rapid prototyping, experience prototyping, visual prototypes, and many others. But the more meaningful conversation revolves around how we actually use those prototypes as a learning tool to quickly get information. We often create a 'primitive form' of something, just to get it out of our heads and actually 'experience' it. Bringing an idea or sketch into the three dimensional world changes it. The key is to find out how it changes and to do so sooner rather than later. You can prototype just about anything. In most cases, you can make a first attempt at a product using whaever you have laying around. At Bright Innovation, we have a giant trunk of LEGOs that has really come in handy when we're working on ideas. Creating something you can tear down and recreate in seconds is powerful not to mention fun. We never know what that thing will be before they create it. They pass it around. They move parts. They pull pieces from it and replace them. They create in real time."
("Rapid Prototyping for Faster Innovation, The story of design by Bright Innovation", http://storyofdesign.com/2011/04/25/rapid-prototyping-for-faster-innovation)

So, the first step in getting control over your finances is to apply this simple investigative/analytical thinking process I will call "Intellectual Prototyping."

It is "intellectual" because you do it in your mind—and with a notebook. It is a thought game, and it is "prototyping" because the spirit of this exercise is to "play" and "mess around" and "get the lay of the land." Prototyping is to build a cheap, quick, risk-free model or mockup of what it is you are thinking of making, and then using that model or mockup to think with. Engineers and scientists do prototyping as a significant part of designing new things.

It is like a golfer on the green, squatting down to "eye ball" the putt before taking it. Looking at the lay of the grass between the ball and the hole, thinking about how hard to stroke the ball to get it to the hole, considering the wind, the tilt of the ground, the "speed" of the grass (length, wetness or dryness, thickness), etc. Like the golfer, before you act, play out the action in your mind fully and completely, living it from beginning to end, so you anticipate as many of the factors at play on the action as possible. "Scope it out!"

Intellectual prototyping for our purposes is an activity you will perform with each of the steps in the chapters to follow.

So, what is the process? Here are the steps of intellectual prototyping:

bound
notebook

1. Get a BOUND notebook of lined but blank paper (not a pad of yellow paper, not separate pages, not Post-It Notes—a BOUND notebook). The cheap ones at the discount stores with mottled black/white covers and about 100 pages are perfect.

    This is your "brain" as you conduct your intellectual prototyping, your collection place of ideas, facts, phone numbers, human sources, websites, gurus, notes, insights, article and book titles and locations, possible solutions or directions, and all other ideas and information that you encounter in your intellectual prototyping. You will "off load" your mind continuously into this notebook while you are doing your intellectual prototyping. If you get something printed out, cut out the text and Scotch tape it into your notebook. This is your primary "thinking tool" for this work. You know that once you get it into your notebook; it is in your system and can be easily retrieved and used for analysis at any time.

on the first
page, write
down
the topic

2. Now, write down on the first page your topic—building a budget, personal finance, how to control finances, or something like that for the next chapter in this book.

   Write down also everything you know now about this subject. What do I want to do or know? What is involved? How do I go about it? What do I have to do first? Are there any rules or laws or things I need to know about first? Do I know anybody who knows about this? Those kinds of things you already know or wonder about. This is your baseline of you successful? Why didn't it work out for you? How do you feel about it? What worries or scares you? What do you feel are the constraints or limiting forces that might keep you from succeeding? Get it all down and out of you.

take your time

to search

↓ write down
information

3. Now, go out far and wide to begin "finding and chasing your cattle" or information towards your answer or solution. Start with a few hours on the Internet searching and reading and taking notes. Be sure to list the URL on any information you feel is important enough to write down, so you can come back to it for more later on. What are you finding? What are the steps people are saying are important? Are you seeing commonalities among the various website presentations on the subject? Do you find any gurus that everyone else refers to? Write down your impressions. Write down books that people recommend. Write down websites or people that seem to be important to others.

go to a bookstore and just sit for a while and scan through all of the books on the shelves on the subject

4. Now, change your search environment. Go to a bookstore and just sit for a while and scan through all of the books on the shelves on the subject. What do they seem to have in common? Write down your thoughts. What are some good ideas? Write them down in your notebook, being very careful to write down the name of the author, the name of the book, and the copyright date, so you have a sense of how recent (often the most intriguing) is the information.

go to foodcourt & start reading your notes

5. Go to the local mall to the food court, get a great big soda, and then go to the eating area off in the corner away from everyone. For this exercise, make this just you, alone. Start reading your notes and thinking about what you have written down. So, what about budgeting? What are the steps? What seems to be the most successful approaches? What makes the most sense to you? What do you see as practical enough for you to implement and stick with? Play around on a blank page in your notebook with an implementation plan: step 1, step 2, step 3, etc.

invite friends and share ideas

6. Now, invite two or three good friends to join you at your table in the food court. Share your ideas. Show them what you have found. Talk it through. Explain to them your implementation plan. Get them to give you their thoughts and ideas. WRITE THEM DOWN AS THEY GIVE THEM TO YOU. Talk, write, think, draw pictures, talk, write, think. Over and over, talk it, think it, get some new directions and new approaches to think about.

remember
YOU HAVE TIME.
SLOW AND STEADY
WINS
THE RACE

7. Remember, you have time. Slow and steady wins the race. Now, do these steps again— and again, and again, until the subject is straight and clear in your mind, until you understand what is being asked of you and you know exactly how to proceed.

write down final
prototyping

8. Write down your final prototyping plan (knowing that things will change and you will have to adjust as you proceed), and get to work on accomplishing the task.

REMEMBER THAT WINNING IS JUST CAUSE AND EFFECT AT WORK!

The idea of prototyping, or thinking through the idea of "making more money" and then how you get control over that money, is great.

Let's see prototyping in action. Many families live paycheck to paycheck and would like to make an extra $300-$500 per month but are just not sure "how" to do this, especially when both the man and woman are working 9 to 5 jobs. This is where prototyping ideas of a "home-based business" really comes into effect.

What do you like to do? What are you passionate about? What products would support your passion? Think of ideas sharing products or services that you get passionate about. What makes you feel great? What makes you smile when you think about being able to share these types of items with others to help them overcome obstacles they have in their life?

Like Zig Ziglar says, "If you help enough other people get what THEY want, you will always get what you want."

In the United States, the government has tax incentives to help small/

home-based businesses start and grow. By helping the small or home business owners keep more of the money they make in their 9 to 5 job and are paying in taxes on each paycheck, which can provide an extra $200-500 per month for the average person, allows them to have the extra income to start and run their own home business and grow it. See, at the end, your goals and the government's goals are both the same: to help you start and grow your home business into a money-making machine, because you then pay more in taxes but you're happy you are as you make more money!

So many individuals get overwhelmed by thinking about how to start making extra money each month, being able to manage their money and track it, or where to invest their money for their future.

Always start by prototyping and getting all the best information out of your head, researched, and documented so you can make powerful and clear decisions.

In this chapter, you learned:

- Recording something on paper can make or break your results.
- You never have to go it alone; research is one of your best friends.
- You have everything you need to create your own budget and plan.
- Prototyping can get you from here to there.

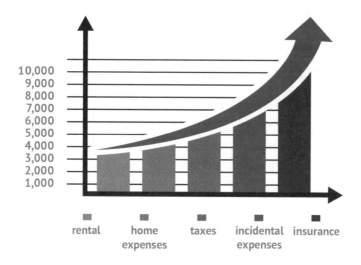

rental	home expenses	taxes	incidental expenses	insurance

IV. Analyze Your Current Financial Situation

Ready with your intellectual prototyping assignment?

I hope you had a good time while working on your ideas. In fact, I believe that intellectual prototyping is sheer fun. I do it all the time. I believe that people should be comfortable with working on new ideas, because ideas push us forward and make our lives better. (Can you imagine mankind without ideas, plans and goals? It would be horrible.)

Of course, you will not be able to carry out all of those great ideas that you have just noted—at least not at once, not right now. And that's okay. But you will always have something to plan, to prepare, to look forward to. And that's great! That little bound book you've just begun to use will remind you every day that your professional life is full of sense and passion. That little book will guarantee that your family life will no longer suffer from the stress and strain of not having money and of living month to month. That little book is your key to freedom. Never forget this.

Now let's get one step closer to your ultimate goal: financial security!

Now that you have learned the method of intellectual prototyping, you are ready to fly.

In this chapter, I will teach you to analyze your current financial situation. I will teach you how to do it step by step. Please follow all the steps, one by one, and do not skip anything.

You might think that you so do not need this, that you know everything about your financial situation... You might think that you have no debt, and since you make ends meet, you have nothing to analyze... You might think that things are as clear as a bell...

But dear friend, please, try to surmount the temptation. Do not rush through this chapter. By the end of it, you will see that analyzing your current financial situation is much more than knowing what comes in and goes out of your budget.

Remember? Slow and steady wins the race! I cannot repeat this enough. So please, do not skip this chapter even if you think you know everything; I might have a surprise (or two) in store for you too.

How do you start the analysis?

First of all, clear your schedule for at least two or three hours. Do this analysis at home, or in your office. Wherever you decide to do it, keep your most important documents, papers, contracts close so you can check things, numbers, debts, etc. out if you have to (and you will have to).

Then make yourself a coffee, close the door, and get started.

Your first and priority task is to decide that you will be brutally honest with yourself. Promise yourself, instantly, that you will hide nothing, and that in turn you will not hide from anything.

The sad truth is that most people do not analyze their financial situation because they are afraid of what they might find as a result. It is only logical and so very human; the self needs a reassurance that things are okay, that the situation is not that bad. The self needs a reassurance that it is part of a good person. As a result, most people hide from the truth and lie to themselves (all the while hoping that the truth will not come to bite them in the ... you know what).

Try not to be one of those people. Be one of those brave guys or gals who are able to be honest with themselves. Be one of those people who are able to look the monster in the eye—and ultimately make it suffer. (And if your financial situation is a fairy tale, be one of those people who embrace it as it is and make it even better!)

Keep your goal in mind

The exercise of analysis is important because you have a goal. Your goal is to obtain financial security to live a happy life, to raise your kids in stability, to be able to stand strong against the financial storms that inevitably blow.

Imagine that you are a great warrior who goes off to conquer the world and create the empire of financial stability. This warrior and his état-major surely needs to know where he stands, what the odds are, and what the troops need in order to successfully carry out the task. You have to know, exactly, your means, your needs, your odds, and your duties in order to be successful. Wanting to conquer, wanting to achieve financial stability is not enough. Dreaming is not enough; that is the business of the 99% who struggle day in day out. Action and preparedness is the prerogative of those warriors who know where they are going, what they want and who are ready to make an effort.

Okay, now how about this comparison? Would you start cooking without assembling all the materials that you need? Surely you do check out the cupboards before you decide to do a chili con carne!

Surely you do read the recipe if you do not know it by heart! Surely you take a look at the kitchen to know whether you have corn, beans and meat in stock! And if you do not have all these things, surely you go to the store. And that is alright. That's how it needs to be. Warriors are like cooks.

INVENTORY

- ☑ **Your current income.**
- ☑ **How many income sources do you have ?**
- ☑ **Weekly paychecks**
- ☑ **Rental fees**
- ☑ **Taxes**
- ☑ **Medical Expences**
- ☑ **Home Expenses**
- ☑ **Leases**
- ☑ **Incidental income**
- ☑ **Statements of account**

The inventory

Okay, so you are sitting there, ready to do the analysis, ready to make that effort, to be that brave warrior (or chef). You have already accepted that this exercise is necessary and you are ready; you want to know where to start, right this moment.

So let me indulge you!

Take a piece of paper (or even better, use the book that you have used for the intellectual prototyping process).

At first, note the following things:

- Your current income. How many income sources do you (or your family) rely on? One? Two? Multiple? Note all the income that you might (usually) come by. Weekly paychecks, rental fees, leases, alimony from your ex-husband. Note it.

- Incidental income. Note anything that you might receive irregularly. Just to take stock of everything.
- Check your statements of account and do not leave anything out.
- Are you cruising on eBay selling this and that? Mark that income, too. You know the drill: brutal honesty.

Now that you have taken a look at the cupboard (you know, what you currently have to cook with), open another page, and begin to mark your current (usual) spendings. The current expenses table / list should obligatorily include the following things and services:

- Rent (if you live in a rented house or flat)
- Mortgage(s)
- Home expenses (water, gas, electricity)
- Leasing contracts and obligations (the monthly cost of your car or cars, for instance)
- Insurance prices (health coverage, life insurance, car insurance, home insurance, etc.)
- Other medical expenses
- Gas, oil, transportation
- Telephone, Internet, cell phones
- Sums transferred to pension funds (if applicable)
- Food and drinks
- Taxes
- Cinema, theater, buying books and other pastime expenses
- Incidental expenses (coffee bought in the coffee shop, pizza orders, etc.)

I know that you know that the next step will be the comparison of your income and of your expenses. And we will get to it shortly.

But we should stop here for a minute.

You have got a table or a list of your expenses. The result actually might surprise you. I hope it will.

How much money do you spend on coffee in a month? How many times do you go out to eat or order in just because you do not feel like cooking?

As you sit there, looking at those lists and tables, start to come to terms with the fact that your budget is not that horrible; you just have to pay attention and work on it every day. If your current income would remain intact, and you could save 2 dollars a day, wouldn't it be huge at the end of the month? Indeed, it would. Or even better: 60 dollars a month is 720 dollars a year, isn't it? (Remember? Slow and steady wins the race!) So, why don't you make that coffee at home in the morning and take it to the office? Is it obligatory to order in three times a week? Come to think of it, is it obligatory to smoke one pack of cigarettes a day?

See, this is the main reason why most people do not bother to do this analysis; if they would be brutally honest with themselves, they would understand that money is just slipping through their hands.

Granted, this analysis is a frightening experience. If you are properly frightened now, that's alright. It means that you have been brutally honest with yourself, and I am very proud of you! That was a huge step and you just took it. Congratulations!

One more word of advice before we go back to your math: You might feel that I am trying to talk you out of things that you love—no. You might feel that I am trying to talk you out of things that spice up your life, without which life would be dull and boring. But this is so not the case.

I am only telling you to count and to do things consciously. If you feel that you can't make do without, that your life would be absolutely miserable without the Starbucks coffee that you drink every morning, or the pizza that you order twice a week, AND if you can afford it, then by all means, continue to drink and eat those items. But be conscious, know how much they cost you, and plan for them in your budget (or "plan" as I like to call it).

And now, let us get back to the inventory of your incomes and expenses.

As you might have correctly guessed, you should compare the two final figures, your income(s) and your expenses by subtracting your expenses from your income(s). Got it? If you are in the green zone, you have less to worry about. However, if you are in the red zone, that means that you regularly spend more than what you earn, that you live way above your means. If that is the case, you really SHOULD (and yes, here I am going to be brutally honest, too: you ABSOLUTELY SHOULD) cut back on the coffee, the cigarettes and the pizza. But I will get to that later, too. Promise.

The debt issue

If you are in the red, it is most probable that you have a huge load of debt, too, because spending—regularly—more than what you earn is not possible without spending someone else's money. (People in the green zone might have debts like mortgages and car leases, so they should not skip the debt part either.)

Therefore, now that you know what you earn and what you spend, it is time to know what you owe.

In order to do so, create a list of your liabilities, and do not forget to note not only the total sum that you owe, but also the annuities and the interest rates. The latter two will be important later, when I talk about getting you out of debt. Just to make sure that you do not miss anything: note your mortgages, home loans, student loans, credit card debts, leases,consumer credits and private debts. Yes, those 200 bucks you owe your mother—note them also.

What you have

Now let's leave the debt where it is now. We are off to happier subjects for a brief moment.

Now I am going to talk about what you have, what you actually own: your assets. You will need to create another list for that. We are going to make an inventory of where you are now in terms of wealth. Note the following assets, and actually try to guess their current value in terms of US dollars and note that sum too (if you have no idea concerning the value of a particular asset, do a quick search on the Internet just to have a vague idea):

- Immovable estate (house, lake house, cabin, apartment, any other vacation property or secondary residence)
- Vehicles that you 100% own
- Checking accounts, saving accounts, cash
- Investments (shares, bonds, bond-funds, securities, stocks, stock-funds, etc.)
- Companies that you own or co-own
- Special savings for retirement (401(k), IRAs, etc.)
- College funds
- Art, jewelry, furnishings

Done? We hope you did not forget to note the estimated value of these assets. It is important! Why?

Because now we are going to calculate your net worth.

The formula is quite simple: you add up your assets and your liabilities separately, and then you subtract the liabilities from the assets.

If you do not want to do this on paper, try one of these on line calculators:

CNN – (See resources page)

Bankrate

Done? Okay.

Now, the result can be any number. Do not sweat it if it is negative for now. Do not sweat it if it is smaller than you would have thought.

Remember? Slow and steady wins the race.Remember?

Brutal honesty.

You are at the beginning of a great journey, and I can promise you here and now that your number will be higher and better next year (you will want to do the math again, promise). Because you are about to take control of your finances and you are about to create the financial security for you and your family that you have always dreamed of.

"Just one more thing"

I have to admit that I just love Lt. Columbo. He has a unique and intelligent style. But that is not the reason why I mention him here. Do you remember the scenes when he just turns around, looks at a person (usually the perpetrator) and says, oh, "just one more thing"? Normally, those "one more things" are more than important; they will be the key to Columbo solving the mystery.

So here is one more thing from me, and it is quite important, too. I recommend one more exercise before you go on to make order in your financial life, before you go practical. This is a little psychological exercise for you.

Start your intellectual prototyping again

Pull out the notebook that you used for the intellectual prototyping exercise. When analyzing your financial situation, you must have had many ideas. Here is the possibility to write them down and to get kind of "rid of them." Psychologically, this very important; your ideas should not weigh you down. In fact, when you write them down, you can make sure that they will be there for you later, but you do not have to keep them in your mind (and eventually be afraid of forgetting them).

So, keeping in mind your financial analysis, and everything that you know about intellectual prototyping, think about the following things (again, if you have to):

- Think about the financial problems and constraints that won't let you realize your dreams for the moment. Debts? Other baggage? Write them down and psychologically get rid of them. Let them go. You will have to focus on the future and on your possibilities from now on.

- Now take stock of your professional life. Take stock of where you are. Take stock of everything you have achieved, and everything you want to achieve in the future. Think about your dreams. Think about the things that you have passion for. These things should already figure in your notebook, but make sure that you begin to imagine and visualize yourself doing things that you really love. This will be your guiding light, the wish that will be there as a final goal, along with financial security. Wouldn't you want to live a financially secure life, doing things that you really love—and be able to spend more time with your family and friends, without the anguish of not having money? Of course you would, and you know you have to work for these things. That is why you are here.

- Next step: think of all the positive things that might happen in the next few months in your life. You should not imagine "new" things here; you should rather merely prepare for what is to come: Will you receive money or will you be up for promotion in a few months? If so, note it.

- Then think about all the negative things that you expect to happen in the years to come. Will your parents retire? Will you be required to financially help them? Will your children go to college without scholarship? Will you have to put away money for such purposes? If so, note it too. These problems will have to be a part of your financial planning—without constantly shadowing you.

Finally

Now that you know everything about your financial situation (or almost anything), we can go on to the next step. In the next few chapters, we are going to begin the work, the adventure of making order in your finances.

In this chapter, you learned:

- You have to be honest with yourself if you want to achieve financial security.
- In order to know where you're going, you have to know where you are. Taking stock of all of your spending and income are integral.
- Purging all of your fears, shame, and other baggage around money by writing about it in your notebook allows you to move forward.

V. How Do You Get Out of the Debt Trap

Debt is bad

The financial crisis of 2008 has become a tragic thing for many Americans. After the fallout, many fellow Americans lost their homes, went bankrupt, and had to start all over again. Many Americans know now that they have to avoid the debt trap and that they have to come out of it as soon as possible if they want to stand strong against the winds of those famous financial storms. Sadly, many Americans had to learn this the hard way. Maybe you are one of them. Maybe not. If not, you can learn one thing from those fellow citizens who lost everything due to the crisis and to their own carelessness: You cannot live beyond your means forever. And you can also learn that consumer debt is a bad, bad thing (who said that you need a second television when you have no money to pay for it in the first place?)

Yes, I am only talking about consumer debt here. If you have a company, a viable business plan, you are profitable, but you cannot develop your business further without taking out a business loan, doing so might do good for your company. I would even encourage you to do so. But in this case, every single dollar that you pay in interest will be compensated by the income and the profit that your company makes. In this case, your debt would be productive—and thus, not necessarily bad. But that second television is anything but productive; it just sucks life and money out of you. If you really want it, wait a year and buy it for cash. But I doubt that you really need a second television that badly anyway.

You can do it!

Many people say that they cannot control their finances because they are up to their eyeballs in debt. That might as well be true, but it is no excuse. I know that the constant feeling of anguish over money can be quite stressful. I know that it can be literally debilitating. If you suffer from this feeling, if you are in debt and do not know how to get out of it, you have just made the single most important step: You have begun to read this book. And I am here to kick you in the right direction; yes, I am here to help you. Let me.

The GREAT news is that you can control your finances if you want to, if you put enough effort into it. It will not be easy or even quick, but you can do it (slow and steady wins the race, never forget that).

The golden rule

The golden rule of getting out of debt is quite simple: live well below your means and reimburse your debts as soon as possible (by using the snowball method that I am going to teach you in just a little bit). Now, you might say that you hardly get by as it is, so how do I want you to live below your means? In fact, the goal of this chapter is to show you that there is a method for that; you can change this situation, though it might require some effort on your part.

You will have to attack debt from two angles: your income and your spending. To put it simply and bluntly, you either have to downgrade your spending or raise your earnings if you want to balance your checkbook again. Alternatively, if possible, you can do both at the same time just to speed things up a little bit...

Take a look at your spending

Remember that I've asked you to record your usual and incidental spending? Remember that I've told you that it would be important later on? Now, that later has arrived.

If you have a list of your spending ready—and I hope that you have—I recommend that you begin to sort the items into three groups: usual spending, unexpected spending that could not have been avoided (like medicine) and unexpected/unplanned spending that could have been avoided.

Got it? Now carefully take a look at all of the columns one by one.

Take a look at your usual spending, like oil and gas, rent and so on. Are there items that you can pull off or substitute? Can you use public transportation instead of your SUV? Can you move to a smaller apartment with a lower rent? Do not exclude any possibility just because it feels uncomfortable or foreign for the moment. Go through the items with quiet detachment and ask the question: "Do I really need this?" Or: "Can I make it less expensive?" You do not have to decide anything right now. Just write down your ideas.

Then move on to the next group of items, your unexpected spending that could not have been avoided. You cannot prepare for being sick, right? However, make sure that you run down that list with the same attention to detail as in the case of your recurrent, usual spending. You might surprise yourself here and there.

And finally, take a look at the spending that could have been avoided. Go on, do the math. Drinking coffee, spirits, cigarettes, dropping by McDonalds, ordering in, going out, partying, indulging your kids when it is not justified, buying things that you don't really need and so on: how much does it cost you every month, and every year?

$2 a day is x per year is x per 2 years,
x per 5,
x per 10,
x per lifetime

Remember, if you can save 2 dollars a day (such a tiny amount of no significance, and who can blame you for that one chai latte, anyway?), that will be 720 dollars at the end of the year.

We would gladly bet that 720 dollars that there are unnecessary items on your list of avoidable spending that you can quite easily get by without. I do not want you to stop doing everything you love, to stop eating everything you like and to stop seeing your friends. But I want you to pay attention to what you are doing. To be conscious about it. For instance, set up a budget for these kinds of things. Put a limit on this spending. Then do not hesitate to note every item you buy, every day. Control your spending in this area, too, and do not let your spending control you.

Take a look at your income

If you have just done things right, you should have been able to find a little breathing room in your budget (if you are able to save money by reducing your spending, instantly begin to "save the savings;" they will be used for the reduction of your debt).

Congratulations, friend, you have just made another important step towards your financial stability!

But if you really are in debt, and I mean up to your eyeballs in debt, controlling your spending will not be enough to make a real change—and I do know it. I know that it is not as simple as that.

I know that in order to make things easier for you, you should also consider raising your income as soon as possible.

At the very beginning of this book, the intellectual prototyping process was partly about finding new ways to raise your income (I hope you did not skip that chapter—if you did, please go back and do that exercise because the whole book and your whole future are based on that methodology).

However, the central idea of intellectual prototyping is creating a home-based business. Of course, building a home-based business takes time, and it will not necessarily raise your income significantly from Monday to Tuesday, nor from Monday to Wednesday. But you need income right away. Therefore, you need to look for a few alternative ways to fill the void until your passion begins to earn you money.

Luckily, there are ways with which you can help yourself more quickly. I will give you a list of a few ideas here, so please feel free to use them extensively. Try as many methods as you want, or as many as you can. Remember, reducing you debt as soon as possible is an indispensable condition for you to be able to realize your dream of financial stability. Never forget that that is your ultimate goal.

Always look towards the financially secure future that waits for you. And you can do it!

Remember: only your goal is important. Nothing else matters. Nothing.

The means is always secondary as long as it is legal and moral. (Ahem: let your means be legal and morally acceptable—at the end of the day, you should be able to look in the mirror, pat yourself on the shoulder and say, "Buddy, you did it!" You can be very, very proud of yourself! Your struggles have paid off!" You cannot do that if your means are … questionable. Stay away from such "solutions.")

A few ideas to raise your income

In a previous exercise, you had to note your usual spendings and your income structure in order to know what you usually need or want to "consume" every month. Then you analyzed those spending in order to know what you can get rid of in order to reduce those spendings. Believe it or not, you can raise your income by substituting those services with other services (like stopping reading "paper-based" newspapers and going online).

Getting out of debt is not always comfortable. I know that. To be honest, the process of attaining financial security is not always comfortable, but it is worth the effort and the sweat. Focus on the result! You might have to spend a little time working overtime, and you might have to change a few habits, but never forget your final goal: financial stability.

Ready for those ideas that might help you to raise your income? Yes? Okay, here we go!

Ways to make money offline:

1. Later on, I will tell you how to establish a home-based business in order to optimize your taxes. However, in reality, establishing a home-based business is not only about taxation. It is also about doing what you are good at, what you are passionate about. Are you an avid photographer? Then go on, take photos, and sell them

as stock photos. Are you good at writing? Then why not write blog posts, guest posts for web sites and blogs? Do what you are good at and enjoy your newfound success and liberty. A freelancing business just might give you the extra income that you need in order to make ends meet. We will get back to this idea more in detail in a later part of the book, so keep it in mind.

home-based business

2. The first and easiest thing that you can do is going through your house, garage, vacation home and car. To put it simply, take a tour and make order around you.

house

garage

vacation house

garden

take a tour and make order around you

Put out the garbage so to speak. This will have a psychological benefit, meaning that if our environment is tidy, we humans also tend to be more collected and more organized. Well, no one likes to live on top of a garbage heap... And yes, take out those boxes that you have been hiding in the attic or the cellar for years. You might ask the question now, "Okay, but what does it have to do with raising my income besides the fact that it will make me more organized?" Good question. The answer is this: you really have to look through everything, every shelf, every pocket, every box, one by one. Because you never know what you find in one pocket, one shelf, one box like this. Many people who have done this tidying up game say that they not only did find valuables (that they could sell for good money) but also good, hard cash, cash, cash. Yep, money as in dollar bills. And that's exactly what you need now, isn't it? So do yourself a favor and do the tour of your immovable properties. See what is hidden there....

3. Speaking of money and selling, take a good look around your environment while you are at it. Do you really need everything? Do you really need that painting? Do you really need that table? Do you really need those ugly porcelains? No? Then why won't you get rid of them? Go and sell them right this instant! In fact, make sure that you sell all the things that you do not need or use regularly. (If you have not used an item for more than a year, it is a safe bet that you will never again touch it.) These unnecessary items might be sold on eBay or any other e-commerce website. Take a few photos and sell all that you can. Also try to get rid of your old books, CDs, DVDs, etc. If you do not read them, do not listen to them, you do not need them. It is as simple as that. If you have time, you might want to visit a second hand bookseller, or a second hand CD and DVD seller; they might buy your stuff instantly so you do not have to work on auctioning them. And that means instant money! Your choice. Also, if you have baby stuff and / or old clothes around that you do not use or have not yet given away, you might want to give selling them a try. Second hand clothes shops exist, too! Be creative, and get rid of everything that you do not need (and everything that you can think of). You will see that you will feel lighter—and your coin purse will be heavier as well. And that is the point....

4. You can offer the same courtesy to other people (neighbors, friends, colleagues) around you. If they have unnecessary objects that they want to sell, offer to do it for them. Ask for a little

commission in case of a successful sale. It is a win-win deal for everyone involved!

win-win deal
for everyone
involved

5. If you are a creative guy or gal, you might want to create little goodies (jewels, little gifts, anything you want or like to do). You can try to sell those handmade items too on eBay and of course other similar sites. And again, offer to do the same thing for others for a small commission. Be a salesman for those who don't know about business, but who have good ideas. Here is another win-win deal for everyone!

sell items
on ebay

6. Many people have foreign currencies lying around in their homes. Did you make a trip to Europe ages ago? Did you participate to a Canadian winter trip last year? If yes, do you still have a few Canadian dollars or euro bills lying around on your shelves? Go on, find them and exchange them. The result might not be a big sum. It will not solve all your problems, but it is money all the same. And now you need every penny you can put your hands on...

you need every
penny you can put
your hands on

7. If you have a free room in your house or apartment, think about renting it to someone. There are always students who look for a place to live, and they would be glad to move to a place that is not that expensive as a separate flat (you rent the room in exchange for services, like babysitting or housework too). There are always tourists who prefer local people and adventure to fancy hotels. Go

and find them if you can. This is a good adventure that might spice up your life a little bit (later, when you are financially stable, you can sign up for a few coach surfing services as well; thus you will be able to travel without paying a lot for your accommodation).

room for rent

8. In fact, rent anything you can think of! Do you have a vacation home? A forest cabin? If you do not use them every day, if you do not live there every day, go and rent them regularly just to make even more money. If you are skillful enough, you can try to rent your tools as well. Why should every habitant of the street buy a lawnmower when they can borrow it from you for a small fee?

*vacation home
*forest cabin

9. If you have long hair, you might want to have it cut because it pays rather well; yes, you have heard that right. There are hairdressers that buy hair in order to create faux hair or hair extensions. Besides, new life, new looks!

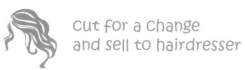
cut for a change
and sell to hairdresser

10. Speaking of extra income: do little jobs whenever and wherever you can. It can be dog walking, taking kids to school, babysitting, lawn mowing, helping elderly people and so on, the list is endless. Be creative. There are many personal services that people are happy to pay for if you can help them to get rid of part of their daily burden.

personal services
job for extra
income

11. Mystery shopping: this one is actually fun. Mystery shoppers are used by companies to check whether their employees adhere to regulations, and whether their internal processes are acceptable, whether they actually work. Sometimes mystery shoppers simply check the quality of a certain service (for example they go to a shop and check whether clerks are polite and professional or rude as hell). So if you need a little pocket money, sign up for a service like this and become a mystery shopper. It will not make you rich, but it might spice up your life a little bit. And who knows, you may get to know people and learn new and fun things...

mystery shopping

12. Do you know how to play the guitar? Play the piano? Do you speak a foreign language? You know how to do something that might interest people? Go on and teach things! Give private lessons. Help kids in difficulty.

private lessons

13. If you are bound to use your car every day, better do it in good company. Share your car with others, and split the expenses. There are car-sharing communities out there; you just have to check out if your city has one or not. And if your neighborhood does not have such an association, go on and create one! You will save loads of money like this; you will make new acquaintances and will have a whole new social circle. Bonus: the environment will love you, too.

split expenses

14. Earning money takes a lot of effort. Creating financial stability requires a lot of effort.

cook good, honest-to-goodness meals

I know it, and now you know it, too. But you are determined. So take care of yourself! Cook good, honest-to-goodness meals at home and take them to your workplace every day. You will see that it will not only instantly save you money, but also raises your spirit. Anyhow, eat better in order to be in good form and ready for the challenge!

Ways to make money online:

1. Take paid online surveys if you have time. Besides the many scam and fraudulent sites, Global Test Market seems to be the most reliable and trustworthy company to turn to. So give it a try, something useful might come out of it.

take online surveys

2. Move to the electronic world as aggressively as you can. For instance, stop reading printed newspapers; use the Internet versions instead. The majority of newspapers let you read their content for free. If that is not the case (the Financial Times, for instance, lets you read a few articles per month for free), the electronic fee is always smaller than the price of the printed version. Choose the electronic version whenever you can. The rule is this: save money where you can, and obviously, here you can. Also, if you use a lot of paper, if you take a lot of notes, think about moving everything to the cloud. Why would you spend a fortune on paper-based notebooks when you have Evernote and other similar services, absolutely for free? Why would you spend on a desk diary when you have dozens of electronic calendars that you can use for free?

If you have a desktop computer, a laptop or a tablet at home, make good use of it, because you can save loads of money by going on line as much as you can. Do not hesitate to do it.

move to electronic world

3. Start a pay-per-click advertising campaign to increase traffic. Pay-per-click advertising, or PPC, is an effective way to maintain a budget for your advertising campaign while driving targeted traffic to your website. What most people like about this form of advertising is that you only pay once someone clicks the ad, hence pay-per-click; you literally get your money's worth. Because there are so many sites available to pick from, you have more choices concerning the amount you wish to pay. However, the more you pay per click, the higher you will appear on the search engine results. Research the different PPC advertising services before joining one. Here is a list of well-known websites that do PPC advertising: Google AdWords, Yahoo, LookSmart, FindWhat, Kanoodle, Enhance, and Search123. With PPC advertising, you can place a limit on how much you want to spend. Basically, you pay for a certain amount of clicks, or visitors, and once the number is reached, the ad will be removed. Because advertising services use keyword search technology, research what keywords are related to your site and use them in the advertisement.

start a pay-per-click advertising

4. Sell your products on your website and research the market. There are many benefits to selling your product/service on your own website: First off, you get to keep all the profits! Because it's your product, you are in complete control of the direction of the company and sales. You set the product price and can change it according to how sales are going. You also get to decide when

to add new products, remove bad ones, and change the product design. The best product/service you can create is one that is related to your expertise or passion. However, don't start making your creation until you do proper research online about the market. Use search engines to see how many related searches are being made on similar products. A good place to do research is on online forums where you can talk about your product. If you don't find many forums about your type of product, then that could mean there is no demand for it. Also ask customers for their opinions about what products they would like by sending your email list a survey, or discussing it on blogs and forums.

 sell your products on your website

5. Submit articles to EzineArticles.com and promote your website. I will use EzineArticles.com as a step-by-step example to discuss how you can submit articles to promote your website.

 submit articles to ezinearticles.com

First, find the section 'Submit Articles' under the "EzineArticles for Authors" segment and fill in the required form of "EzineArticles Membership Account Creation." The following page will contain specific questions about the article. Choose the category and subcategory of your article from a drop menu in the "Select a Category: Subcategory" section, and then fill in the "Article Title." Next is the summary of the article, which is what readers see first and will continue reading the full article if they are interested. "Article Body" is where you submit the actual article. Under "Author Bio-SIG-Resource Box," you should provide a link to your site, and can even offer a free bonus for visitors. For "Keywords," provide keywords so the search engine can direct people to your article. Once EzineArticles reviews the article, it will be added to their system. Your website will be promoted through both the article itself and EzineArticles' archive of all the sites provided. Also, if other websites or newsletter suppliers want to use your article, they will have to keep the resource box that has your website link.

6. Study the market and find the most profitable products. You don't want to sell products that, well, can't sell!! Do some research about your niche to find out what the most profitable market is. As you become an expert in your field, you will learn what your customers' interests are. Research your target customers' needs and wants so you can show them how your product/service can be of benefit to them. Don't just advertise; always show customers how they can benefit personally. Do research on your product ideas to see if it already exists on the market. You should also visit the sites that sell similar products and check out your competition. By seeing what they provide, you can be a step ahead by offering additional benefits. Research the market by looking over related sponsored advertisements. If there are many ads, then sellers are making money from that niche. Another way to get an idea of the market demand is to find out how many searches are made for keywords involving your market, and the estimate price advertisers are paying per click for ads using these key terms.

 study the market and find the most profitable products

7. Offer good customer service and make more sales online. If you want to start a successful online business, there are a couple of tips to remember in order to be prepared to provide customer satisfaction, because most profits will come from repeat customers and not random visitors. Put effort into providing excellent customer service; that means having a contact page available and responding to e-mails fast. Keep in mind, word of mouth provides the best promotion! For an effective business, have a central distribution for your products and always check that that your web inventory is full. Provide more than one payment option so

you don't limit your customer base. Also put up a shopping cart program so customers can buy multiple items at a time. Don't confuse buyers on your page; provide clear instructions on how to order, or supply a call to action, like "Click here to order." Give potential customers a reason to buy by offering a money back guarantee, bonus item, or trial sample to try first. It is also good to display real life testimonials from people who bought the product and liked it.

 good customer service and sales online

8. Distribute press releases to media and offer valuable information. You can increase your web traffic and sales though press releases. This internet marketing tool will go a long way if you provide newsworthy information, and target it to the appropriate media outlets. Press releases should include information that audiences would be interested in. Editors are concerned with finding news that is informative, not advertisements for your personal gain. Your press release should look professional, and be only a page long. Place a heading on top of your company letterhead that states "New Release" or "For Immediate Release." Provide contact information at the top including your name, company, address, phone, fax, e-mail address, and website. Below this, write a descriptive headline that will attract the attention of readers. Body content should state product/service benefits immediately to keep readers interested, and because editors usually cut from the bottom of a press release if they need to shorten it. Emphasize how your product/service can solve a problem or achieve a goal for customers. Always give readers follow-up information so they can reach you, and perhaps offer a free bonus, like an e-book.

 distribute press release to media

9. Submit articles to directories and link back to your website. You can submit your articles to several online directories. These websites usually have articles on many different topics with authors from across the world, so you shouldn't have a problem finding a directory for your article. To get published, you will need an interesting topic that people want to read about. Writing about a specific niche you specialize in will help you get recognition as an expert. Articles (as opposed to ads) are more personal, so you will also be building stronger relationships with readers. Make sure your articles have a catchy title so readers will be interested in what else you have to offer. At the end of each article, you can provide information about yourself, as well as a link back to your website in the resource box, which gives you a chance to drive traffic in to your site. Article marketing will also benefit your page rank, as search engines will see you as a good source of information. Provide links to your articles through your website too so visitors have a chance to read them.

submit to directories and link back to your website

10. Create a new product/service and start an affiliate program. If you have an idea for a product/service, search the internet for any sites that might have something similar. If your idea is totally original, not only can you introduce a new product/service to the market, but you can make large profits by starting an affiliate program. To increase sales, you should guide your affiliates with your marketing techniques on how to promote your product, and provide them with promotional tools. This is a win-win situation, as you are profiting by helping others sell your items, and they are gaining quality assistance and advice. Start an e-mailing list for your affiliates. Update them on any new products you launch or send them alternative advertising material. Keep the niche of your affiliate program related and organized.

create new
product &
services

Find websites that have the same niche, and offer them your affiliate program. This way you can be advertised on pages where visitors are likely to be your target customers. Give them an attractive offer by showing them how your websites are complementary, and can mutually benefit each other.

11. Sell coaching programs and offer your skilled advice. You don't actually have to sell hard information products to customers; instead, you can sell training information, such as coaching products. If you are an expert in a field, such as advertising, you can host coaching programs on teleseminars where people pay you to review their advertising material. This takes the form of a discussion with a group of people, as ideas go back and forth between you. Basically, you can use your skills to provide useful criticism and feedback. Other coaching programs come in the form of group participation programs, like a weight loss teleseminar, where the people who sign up come together to share their stories, experiences, and advice. Coaching products are not necessarily held in discussion groups; they can be a live lecture where people can listen in, but not get involved in the program. Alternatively, it can be a live open forum, where discussion and questions are permitted at the end of the program. You can even sell coaching products that are pre-recorded, and just play them over and over for new buyers.

sell coaching
program and offer
your skilled advice

12. Start an online travel agency and build business contacts. People today arrange and book their travel plans through the internet, whether it's for a long vacation or a short trip. There are also many different types of travel agencies, which offer everything

from cruises, to safaris, luxury deals, or simply hotel and flight budget. For those just beginning, it is best to use a daily budget, as you want to be able to stop advertising if they are not bringing in good sales results. Edit your ads so they perform better, and then increase your spending so you seize every opportunity to receive a visitor. In general though, it is best to avoid a monthly budget because search engines can't equally distribute your ads over the whole month. Since they can't determine how many clicks you will receive, you may end up having your ad removed before the end of the month. Take into consideration the best dates to place daily ads, such as the time of month when people get paid, and are willing to spend.

Start online travel agency

13. Write quality blogs on specific niches and sell related products. You can start a blog for many reasons; some use it as a personal online diary to connect with people, but you can also use it as a marketing tool for your website. Alternatively, you can simply start a blog, and earn money off of it directly. Provide readers with useful information related to the topic of your website. Always write about something you are an expert in, or passionate about, as you want readers to trust your content. It will also build your reputation and relationship with readers so that, later on, they will be open to your advice and the recommendations on your website.

Start quality blogs on specific niches

You can make money off the blog itself by hosting related advertisements or allowing sponsored posts. Just make sure that the blog doesn't appear to be only a sales page with no useful content. Articles should be well-written and helpful, not only to catch readers' attention, but also because other people may want to include you on their blog as a guest post. This will get you more and more recognition.

14. Sell items through online auctions and start a profitable business. Before, we used to host garage sales to sell our items, but now online auctions provide an opportunity to sell your items to a larger customer base. These websites, like eBay and Craigslist, give you the chance to sell used items as well as new products. Selling products that are in demand can become your new job! Always stay up to date with the market, and do research to discover what the top-selling items on online auctions are. You can even find resources online, like Terapeak and eBay Pulse, which are websites that help users do research about eBay to discover hot target markets, learn who your competition is, and find the best selling categories. If you are setting up an auction business, you need to find good suppliers so customers are satisfied. It is important that you build a reputation by keeping customers happy, or else people will not maintain a business relationship with you. The more credible you are, the more new customers will trust buying from you. Provide honest descriptions, professional headlines, and trigger words.

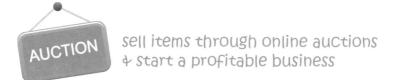

sell items through online auctions & start a profitable business

15. Earn a commission by joining professional affiliate programs. Joining an affiliate program will allow you to earn a commission for every sale that is made by a customer who came through your link. There are many options available online, so take your time; the well-known ones include: Amazon, Ebay and ClickBank. Do research to find the best program for your website, because you want to be selling products/services that are related to your topic and reader interest, not just displaying any unrelated ad that comes your way. Check how well their top affiliates are doing, if this information is provided, so you get an idea of how good the program is. A good tracking mechanism is also needed so you can keep record of how well your ads are doing and how much you've

earned. Find a good program that can provide you with tools to sell their product including banners, text links, and graphics that you can display on your website.

earn by joining professional affiliate programs

The program should also have an attractive website, as they are the ones that will need to make the sale after you send the customers to them.

16. Become an eBay "Trading Assistant" and sell other people's items. There are many people who don't know how to use eBay and aren't interested in trying, while others simply don't have the time. Whatever the reason, you can make a business from selling these peoples' items! However, you need to research the product first to see if it will sell, and inform the client of the pricing range. Make sure it makes enough money to pay your fees and benefit your customer. As a "trading assistant" for other people's goods, as eBay calls them, you need to keep the item with you for as long as the auction/bid is open. It is your responsibility to take a picture of it, write its listing, handle the payment transaction, and then provide the shipping. Any fees you need to pay in the process should be charged to the owner of the item. Discuss all charges with your client beforehand so nothing comes out of your pocket. Although you can start an eBay business from home, some people become so successful that they open actual stores where items can be dropped off!

become an ebay "trading assistant"

17. Buy products with resale rights and earn the whole profit. Buying products that offer resale rights provides you the chance to earn full profit from reselling without paying any percentage to the original owner. Newer resale products are usually more profitable,

because older products are commonplace in many of your competitors' sites. Do a check on search engines to estimate its value. Find resell packages that are related to your website, have high-quality content, provide pre-made pages and professional sales copy, and perhaps offer a sales bonus that you can use to attract customers to buy. Some businesses offer Master Resale Rights, allowing you to not only resell a product, but to offer your customers the right to resell as well. This will add value to your product. Some information products offer Private Label Rights, which basically allows you to change the content, put yourself as the author, and alter the name of the product. But always check if there are any restrictions on the reseller license. Some packages have restrictions on the minimum price of the resell, while others don't allow resell products to be used as a bonus item.

buy products with resale rights and earn the whole profit

Evidently, you do not have to apply all these income-raising methods at once. These are just examples that you can begin with. Perhaps you will have other creative ideas. You might want to go back to your intellectual prototyping book and spend a little time thinking about it. I think it would be a good thing. Go on, I will be here waiting for you. Come back with new ideas soon!

Now, let's start to get you out of debt!

Remember our mantra: slow and steady wins the race.

Getting out of debt is not always a quick process, but there are methods with which you can make it a rather spectacular process. If you are stressed by your debts, chances are that you will enjoy seeing them shrinking. I would. And I can promise that you will, too.

By the way, by analyzing your incomes and spending, you have just made an important step towards getting rid of your debt. You know why?

If all went well above, you must have found by now a little wiggle room in your budget, and / or you must have many ideas as to how to raise your income. The good news is that we will use all that newfound money to lower your debt, and ultimately to get rid of your debt in a spectacular way. I'll get to that in a moment.

However, first, you need to commit to the change. You need to decide right now that you want to get rid of debt for once and for all. Imagine yourself debt-free and happy, and financially secure. Visualize yourself in that blissful state of mind. (Don't forget, financial prosperity begins with attitude.)

Now, find a moment to take a look at all of your loans, consumer credits and their terms of service. Think about refinancing. Think about replacing your existing obligations with others that offer you better terms and conditions. A 3-percent difference in the interest rate might mean 30-percent change in your annuities, so it is absolutely worth it to look for refinancing opportunities! Yes, call banks and look actively for better opportunities every day. Meanwhile, just for the fun of it, call your own service provider every day if you need to; you never know when they will offer you better terms!

Done with that? Cool. (I hope you noticed that you cannot be "done" with something you have to do every day!)

Now I am going to teach you the infamous snowball method so that you can get out of debt relatively quickly (okay, by "quickly" here I rather mean "spectacularly," but never mind, go on).

The snowball method is all about psychology and attitude (as everything I talk about in this book), and I think that you know by now without me reminding you that I believe that financial prosperity is also about psychology and attitude.

The snowball method is more than that though; yes, it needs commitment, but it will help you not only to get you out of debt, but also to enjoy it as a great personal success! Yes, you will like it, because its results are so spectacular.

I hope that you are curious and ready for action.

Here is how to do it:

1. First of all, make a list of all of your debts, credits cards, consumer loans, student loans and so on. Do not miss a thing. If you have done our previous exercises correctly and properly, if you have finished most notably the one where you had to evaluate your current financial situation and calculate your net worth, you must have that list right there on your table. Got it? Okay.

2. Now, you will have to organize that list according to balance. The loan with the least balance comes first, and the loan / debt with the greatest balance comes last.

3. Got that organized list? Just checking. If not, go on, write it down; I am waiting.

4. Okay, here is the deal: you will have to continue to pay all your balances, but always the minimum.

5. With one exception: the first debt with the least balance.

6. As in previous exercises you have already decided to raise your income or lower your spendings, so you have that wiggle room that you need in order to start the snowball rolling. 50 dollars a month? 100 dollars per month? 200 dollars a month? 1000 dollars a month? The sum does not matter as long as it is explicitly saved in order for you to pay your debt off. Of course, make it as much as you can; the more you have, the quicker the process will be.

7. So you are going to use that "wiggle room" money, every month to prepay your first debt with the least balance. (You can check out the terms and conditions for prepayment, but

many service providers do not charge extra for that. If they do, simply save the money in a savings account and prepay a big sum all at once.)

8. When you are done with the first debt with the least balance, you go on to the second. You take all the money that you have used while paying off the first debt, and add it to the payments of the second debt.

9. When the second debt is paid, you take, again, ALL OF THE MONEY that you used to pay it off, and move on to the third debt. As you get rid of your debts one by one, you will always use more and more money to pay the next one off: the sum will grow like a snowball.

This is a popular, and very clever method, because the results are so visible and so spectacular. This method raises your spirit, fuels your psyche and gives you hope. Yes, you can, just to plagiarize our sitting President.

Yes, beyond doubt, this is a spectacular method and I recommend it earnestly. Do it. Do not hesitate. **You are the only one who can get you out of that mess you are in. And you will.**

P.S. There is a second version of the snowball method, where debts are listed according to their interest rates. Indeed, it might be cheaper to list your debts according to interest rates. However, the version that I have presented above is more encouraging psychologically. And remember, this is all about attitude and psychology.

In this chapter, you learned:

*   You have two options for getting yourself out of debt: earning more and spending less. Doing these two things in sync will create the best results.

*   Be conscious about your debt. Don't ignore it because it feels overwhelming. You do have the power to handle this.

- There are many options to make more money, both online and off.

- Tools like refinancing and snowballing can make a huge difference in your debt management.

Understanding MONEY adds a positive dimension to WEALTH

VI. Establish Control Over Your Finances

"Money, by itself, is neither good nor bad—it's neutral. Money is an energy tool. Like a hammer, money can be used to build or to destroy. We believe that understanding money—how to ethically make it, keep it, and share it—adds a positive dimension to wealth. Our lives, our relationships, and our happiness improve when we have enough money. That's why we wrote this book. Money properly earned and combined with enlightened intentions makes the world a better place." (Hansen/Allan, The One-Minutes Millionaire, ii)

In this chapter, you will learn about creating spending plans and taxes, and you will put in place your own money management process and spending plan and establish a home-based business.

Remember:

1. Take a deep breath; you can do it. You have the attitude and the commitment, and you now have momentum going for you to

get these things done.

2. Slow down, take another deep breath; you know how to go about thinking and prototyping to get this subject under control and to formulate an implementation plan. You know exactly how to "gather your cattle" or ideas up and to massage and work them down into a meaningful plan. You know how to use your notebook to capture information, to off-load it from your mind, and to organize it.

3. Now, as a kind of footnote to this and the work in the next few chapters, you need to get a secure place, like a safe or a fire-/water-proof container or box into which you will put these personal and, sometimes, legal financial documents.

Now, let's talk about creating spending plans and taxes.

As you begin to build for prosperity and financial security, there are two basics you need to take care of at the beginning. (1) You need to establish a spending plan and stick to it, and (2) you need to establish a home-based business to control your taxes.

As you probably have noticed, I don't use the word "budget"… I think people feel that word is restrictive, time consuming and boring. I like to establish "spending plans." Everyone likes to "spend;" now I show you how to spend with purpose.

Establish a spending plan and stick to it

"If you're like most people, the lack of planning and budgeting is precisely the problem. It's boring. It's a hassle and time-consuming."
(Solin, The Smartest Money Book, xii)

"Budgeting is not a dirty word. Fiscal responsibility is like monogamy … if you think it's boring, you're doing it wrong….Think of 'budget' as just another word to say edit."
(Hoffman, Bitches on a Budget, 3)

This is going to be a very short discussion because web-hosted, bank-sponsored, and a myriad off-the-shelf packages give excellent budgeting and expense tracking programs or applications. Creating spending plans has become so simple and intuitive, especially with the great technologies of this day, that you just need to buy the program or get online, signup and pay the fee, and engage earnestly and intensely with it. You can easily and quickly get control over your money.

Remember, as you get going here to have your notebook ready to record where you go and what you think and learn. Always begin by looking everywhere, as far and wide as possible, and writing it down, so you get the best possible sense of creating a spending plan, home-based business, and taxes. Start filling pages in your notebook.

The expense and money management system I recommend as a good solution for you is named The Expense Tracker (www.TheExpenseTracker.com). Of course, I recommend you look around, fill your notebook with alternatives, and consider ALL possible Money Management tools. I hope your exposure to The Expense Tracker will help form a baseline for you for comparison/ contrast and deeper evaluation of all of the alternatives out there.

THE
EXPENSE TRACKER
LIVE RICH. SPEND SMART.

Pause now and go to the website www.theexpensetracker.com. You will need to pay the small fee to get going, but that is minimal compared to the value of the discipline of theprogram. So, sign up, click around in the program, and start learning the program and using it with your own data.

Shown to the right is the landing page for this website so you will recognize it.

Spend an hour or so just clicking on the various parts of the website. Read and come to understand what the program offers.

The system is simple; it gives you a "typical" list of expenses and "other" fields you can customize. It auto-populates a spending plan for you to help you get started in less than 5 minutes. You then enter changes to customize the system to your situation.

The system is voice, text, and APP based, so you can enter your expenses easily and intuitively. It enters changes and updates the accounts immediately while giving you balance updates by category anytime, anywhere, on any device.

They have also included a pre-paid debit card/MasterCard. This allows you to set the amount you want to spend on the debit card/MasterCard, and when you spend, it auto-categorizes the expense and stops you with your pre-determined limit. This helps individuals that have a hard time sticking to a spending plan.

You see your financial situation displayed in detail in front of you at all times via online or mobile, so you see the results of your actions.

However, you will choose the solution that works best for you after you have done your prototyping and thinking search and analysis. Whatever solution you choose, I recommend that you use it 'religiously' for at least three months so you make sure you are gaining the discipline you need to control your money. After this "eye opening" period, you will see the discipline paying off for you, as your available money builds and your expenses come under control.

That's it. Probably the most difficult and most dreaded aspect of building for prosperity and financial security is creating a spending plan and the discipline and control that surround that activity. When you use a tool like The Expense Tracker the task becomes simple and intuitive. It makes it manageable, and therefore simple. And if it's simple, you're more likely to do it. Your action leads to consequences, and when you consistently use a tool like The Expense Tracker, you get the consequences you want.

In this chapter, you learned:

- Keep your financial information in a fireproof, waterproof container for safe keeping.

- One of the keys to success is making a plan and sticking to it. Using a tool like The Expense Tracker can make this very easy for you.

- You must be consistent. Track, track, track.

VII. Establish a Home-Based Business to Control Taxes

"Ordinary and necessary" business expenses

Typically, all "ordinary and necessary" business expenses can be deducted from your business income when filing your business tax return. Such deductions may include business travel, office and/or computer equipment, attorney and accounting fees, delivery costs, utilities, and rent. These are items that are necessary to properly conduct your business. Mileage accrued for business-related travel can also be deducted at the current rate of $0.56 per mile. (The Expense Tracker tracks mileage automatically via phones GPS).

Keep a careful record of your expenses, and have backup material on hand for documentation whenever possible. If you have incurred expenses that are both business and personal in nature, such as a trip that was for both business and personal reasons, you can deduct a portion of those expenses. Use discretion when determining what portion of the total expense was business-related. Make sure to document all such expenses.

The steady rise in home-based businesses has created some gray areas regarding business deductions. As is generally the case, you need to be able to justify each deduction in the event a tax auditor should question it. If you conduct business from a home-based office, for example, you can claim a deduction for the portion of your home that's being used for business purposes. Accordingly, you can also claim a percentage of your utilities, phone bill, and other related costs such as Internet service used for business purposes. Save your bills, and show the percentage you used as a business expense.

THE
EXPENSE TRACKER
LIVE RICH. SPEND SMART.

For all deductions you'll want to maintain a paper trail including receipts listing the date, name of the person or business receiving the payment, the total amount paid, and the category of business expense, or just use The Expense Tracker's simple phone app that captures this information instantly.

We are seeing today (2014) on the national political stage a discussion of wealth and taxes. This is a wonderful education for most Americans because we are seeing the tax code, the tax laws, the tax strategies of wealthy people as opposed to middle class people, and the positive results of money management. Why do some pay 35% in taxes while others pay 15%? How is it that some know how to make maximum use of the tax code to save taxes and maximize income while others do not? The answer is simple: The more we learn, the more control we can exercise on our own behalf.

"The are two tax systems in America, one for the 'informed' and one for the 'un-informed.'" (Judge Learned Hand)

Here is an example of the two tax systems and how the rich get richer:

This chart is the example for the text

No Tax	Principal	Taxable	35% Tax	Net
1.00	1.00	1.00	0.35	0.65
2.00	1.30	0.65	0.23	1.07
4.00	2.17	1.07	0.38	1.77
8.00	3.54	1.77	0.62	2.92
16.00	5.84	2.92	1.02	4.82
32.00	9.64	4.82	1.69	7.95
64.00	15.90	7.95	2.78	13.12
128.00	26.23	13.12	4.59	21.64
256.00	43.28	21.64	7.57	35.71
512.00	71.42	35.71	12.50	58.92
1,024.00	117.84	58.92	20.62	97.22
2,048.00	194.44	97.22	34.03	160.41
4,096.00	320.82	160.41	56.14	264.68
8,192.00	529.36	264.68	92.64	436.72
16,384.00	873.44	436.72	152.85	720.59
32,768.00	1,441.18	720.59	252.21	1,188.97
65,536.00	2,377.95	1,188.97	416.14	1,961.81
131,072.00	3,923.62	1,961.81	686.63	3,236.98
262,144.00	6,473.97	3,236.98	1,132.94	5,341.02
524,288.00	10,682.04	5,341.02	1,869.36	8,812.69
1,048,576.00	17,625.37	8,812.69	3,084.44	14,540.93

First, take $1 and double it 20 times:

Doubling without taxes = $1,048,576.00. This is what the rich understand—money compounds!

Now, take the same $1 and double it, but take out taxes (35% tax rate example) = $17,625.37.

$1,048,576.00 vs $17,625.37. This is not trivial!

You are either part of the "informed" or "un-informed." Period. This is the "why" that everyone should own and operate a home business!

This is the difference, and what MOST people don't realize is the more money I keep, the more money I can make for myself. In reality, you and the IRS have the same goal: make more money because you will pay more in taxes, BUT be happy you did because you bring a lot more income home.

You see, we all go to school to learn "how" to make money, but when did we ever learn how to "manage" money and even more, how to "maximize" our money?

The wealthiest people in the world will always say, "minimize your tax liability to the legal minimum."

Because so many people "don't know what they don't know"….taxes are the biggest source of savings instantly for a household.

Fact: 70% of all bankruptcies in America could have been avoided with just an extra $300 in household income.

Until something like our current political conversation reveals economic information, we do go about life in financial ignorance. Many people are learning about "tax strategies" for the first time as they hear the discussions about wealthy people and their finance/tax strategies today. We're learning, for example, of the "Buffett Rule," which addresses the issue of wealthy people paying less tax than their secretaries, and we are learning, maybe for the first time for many, some significant facts about the U.S. tax code and how some people are using it to their maximum advantage.

What can you do today, as a regular American citizen, to take maximum advantage of the tax codes as you work to establish your prosperity and financial security?

I want you to be aware of the value to your financial prosperity and financial security of knowledge of some simple tax code applications to home-based businesses.

Ask most people what their biggest lifetime expense might be, and they'd guess housing (rent or mortgage payments) or maybe even food. The truth is that your biggest lifetime expense is income tax.

The average American family loses about 33 percent of their income to taxes, representing their single largest household cost. Taxation is the single largest obstacle against wealth creation, yet it is also the one major expense that you can control. In fact, the difference between success and failure in your family relationship and family finances can be traced back to whether you are in control of your tax bill or not.

With the government taking away 30 to 40 percent of every dollar you make, you must

Remember, in a home-based business, as you are using it to get control of your finances, cash is king. Accounts receivable and accounts payable control your life.

There are people who prey on anyone who shows that they have money, so keep in mind exactly WHY you are doing a home-based business and protect your cash!

People who physically work hard for money trade their time for money, which the government taxes at the highest rate possible. Employees, who trade time for money, work harder and harder only to be taxed more and more. This vicious hamster wheel cycle can only end when you take control of how taxes affect your income.

minimize your taxes. The tax code actually punishes employees and rewards business owners. The reason for this is to encourage more people to start businesses and to invest, since small businesses help fuel the economy.

Taxes are the reason why employees rarely get wealthy. The theory that you'll be rewarded if you put in a hard day's work is a fairy tale with an unhappy ending. Millions of people work hard every day, and most are not rich or wealthy by any standard.

The simplest and easiest solution to this crushing taxation problem facing most families is to start a home-based business.

Let me be clear—it makes little difference what, exactly, you choose to do in your home-based business as long as it is ethical and has some hope for success. Many people open a local restaurant or services business in their local communities. Others join a multi-level marketing organization that offers products or services. Others might open a counseling or legal or accounting business. Whatever. It doesn't matter for this discussion what it is.

OK, you are probably saying to yourself "where does anyone learn these Tax Strategies, especially when I am working 8-10 hours a day, trying to spend time with family, get a good night's sleep?…When do I have the time?"

I spoke earlier about building a spending plan and a system that makes managing money simple and fun. Specifically, I recommended The Expense Tracker.

One thing that is truly unique about this system is that it partnered with the home-based business tax experts. Because of this partnership, The Expense Tracker created videos on all the tax laws: "Why a home business is a smart financial decision," "Why being an entrepreneur is the lifeblood of the economy," "Why the government gives you these tax incentives and how to maximize them correctly," and many simple quick videos to educate you immediately.

The Expense Tracker also created videos on each business deduction category that you might want to learn about and even allows a tax expert to educate you in real time, on-demand about what you can and cannot do when writing off business deductions for your home business. This makes it so simple and quick to get up to speed on how to maximize your business and your money.

KISS—Keep It Simple, Sweetie!

Yes, of course you can change the world, and yes, of course, you could save the rain forests and prevent global warming and bring about world peace. However, as one oil lube company states, "Some people want to change the world; we just want to change your oil." For most of us struggling to get our finances under control, the simpler the home-based business the better. By doing something simple as your home-based business, something that you can do with the basics, you're more likely to follow through.

With a small room in the home dedicated to the business, with a card table and folding chairs, with a dedicated phone line or a dedicated cell phone, with a good Internet service and a good computer, with good money management software, with a local business license, and with an Internal Revenue Tax number (all with a minimum cash outlay), you are in your home-based business.

When you're an employee collecting a paycheck, the government immediately deducts its 30 to 40 percent of your income. Whatever is left over is yours to spend as you like. Therefore as an employee, you can do nothing to reduce your income tax expenses.

However, the government taxes businesses differently. Where the government gets paid first with every employee paycheck, the government gets paid last with every business. An employee pays taxes first and then uses the remaining money to pay expenses. A business pays expenses first and then uses any remaining money to pay taxes. Building a business allows you to generate income and create enterprise value; however, no amount of cash flow can offset the dramatic effects that taxation can have against wealth creation.

Even though the government may still be taking 30 to 40 percent of a business's profits, the amount of money can be much less.

Suppose you're making $50,000 a year. If the government takes 40 percent of your income ($20,000), that leaves you with $30,000 to pay all your expenses. However, if your business earns $50,000 a year, you pay all your expenses first and anything left over gets taxed at the 30 to 40 percent range. If you had $40,000 in expenses that means you'd only get taxed on the remaining $10,000. Take 40 percent out of that amount and you'll wind up only paying $4,000 in taxes. Can you see how paying $4,000 in taxes is so much less than paying $20,000 in taxes? Now you are beginning to understand.

	Employed with someone else	Self-Employed
Annual Income	$50, 000	$50, 000
Money goes to Goverment (%)	40% (annual income)	30%-40% (annual income)
Money goes to Goverment ($)	$20, 000	$10, 000
Net Income	$30, 000	$40, 000
Tax	$20, 000	$4, 000

So, after you have your spending plan in place to control the handling of the money coming into your home, into your life, now you can start making sure you keep it for your own prosperity and financial security.

Starting a home-based business with the intent to earn a profit is the number one way you can greatly reduce your tax expense. This is not tax evasion (which is illegal), but tax minimization. If you want to reduce your biggest lifetime expense, you cannot afford not to start your own business. Until you can minimize your taxes, you will always be a slave to money and not a master of it.

In this chapter, you learned:

- Home-based businesses can make a huge difference when it comes to tax time.

- When it comes to making the most out of your taxes, knowledge is half the battle.

- You don't need to go all out to have a home-based business. Keep it simple, and you'll see results.

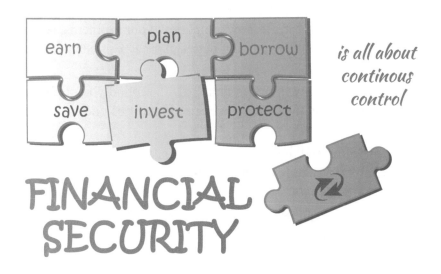

earn   plan   borrow

save   invest   protect

is all about continous control

FINANCIAL SECURITY

VIII. Financial Security is All About Continuous Control

Do you know those (sometimes kind of weird) people who go on and on repeating and repeating the mantra of consciousness? Finances are like breathing. Nothing comes for free these days, so you'd better keep watching your finances like a very conscious hawk!

When it comes to finances, consciousness is the key. You can be aware of your breath, but you can breathe without paying attention to it. However, if you are not aware of your finances, you are doomed to financial failure. You cannot imagine the number of clients who come to me asking for help—and they do not even understand their own financial situation! They know that they are six feet under, they know that they have serious problems, but they do not know the exact parameters of their problems. Come on! It is sometimes unbelievable, even for me.

Dear friend, dear reader, luckily, **you are NOT one of these careless people**. And that is great. By now, you know your problems, so you understand your financial situation better than 99% of people out there.

In fact you know many things in detail. Let's remind you of all we have done so far together since the beginning of this book:

- You know and understand the current structure and the potential structure of your income. You know all the resources that are available to you.

- You have even brainstormed ideas for a quick raise in your income, and with the intellectual prototyping process, you have laid down the basics of your future financial prosperity. Kudos!

- You know (in detail) not only what you earn, but you know what you spend, too.

- You have a list of the things that you can make do without; you understand that sometimes you literally throw money out of the window. You are ready to reconfigure your budget / spending plan.

- You have the means to track your financial development (calculating your net worth every year),

- And you also know a great method to reduce your debt (if you are in debt, of course)

I could say that you have just begun to work on your finances, and you have already done a great deal. Now—and here comes the most important part—what you did once, you need to do all the time!

All the time? Yes. **Controlling and knowing your finances must become a habit of yours.**

Consider this:

"Watch your thoughts, for they become words. Watch your words, for they become actions. Watch your actions, for they become habits. Watch your habits, for they become your character. And watch your character, for it becomes your destiny."

I am sure that somewhere along the line you have heard this famous quote before. Some say that it was the late British PM, Margaret Thatcher, who said it; some say that it was Lao-Tzu, while others claim that some religious prophets are to be considered as the source. It does not matter, though! What matters is the ultimate wisdom behind this quote.

Take a moment to re-read it. If you think that you are poor and that there is no way to stabilize your financial situation, you will always remain poor, because you will not act in order to make the change that is needed. If you believe that you can make that change—and yes, you can!—you will act in order to obtain your goal. And if your actions are pertinent, if you see that they work, that they bring results, they will become your habit. The rest you understand.

You, and only you, control your financial destiny. Not your mother, not your mother-in-law, not your wife, not your husband, not your kids, not your boss, not the IRS, not the President, not the Congress. You and only you. Of course, there is baggage that you might carry around on your back, I reckon. You might not be guilty of creating it. You can be only negligent: your crime then is negligence, not doing what has to be done and what can be done in order to revert your financial destiny.

Therefore, financial attention and financial responsibility need to become part of your habit, and ultimately, your character. One step of a time, you can change your character and you can change your destiny. One step at a time you can become a financially secure person.

Here are the golden rules that you will have to follow each and every day:

- Track your expenses every day. Note every single penny that you spend. Ask your family members to do the same. If they do not cooperate (why wouldn't they?), track the sums that they have control over. Consider them as expenses.

- Track and control your taxes the way we explained above. Cut them any way you can, as long as the method and the results are legal.

- Always live below your possibilities, and save as much money as you can (we will explain the best saving methods later on). When you see something that you really would like to buy, ask yourself the question: do I really need this? Would I buy it if the impulse weren't there?

- Do not use your credit card, unless World War III is about to erupt and you are in grave physical danger... Attention, I do not say that you should get rid of your credit card. Credit cards are not the source of all evil. You can collect, for instance, points with them (and then go for a vacation, a trip, etc. with the points collected; I am all for that!). But make sure that you reimburse the card ahead of time in order to avoid paying interest. Use your cards wisely and do not let them use you!

- Avoid consumer debt (car payments and company) like the plague. Quite simply: do not buy anything you cannot instantly pay for. If you cannot pay for something, it means that you cannot afford it. Period.

- Try to save money for big expenses beforehand and always pay ready cash (thus you save the interests, again, which constitute a huge sum at the end of the day). If you know that your kid will go to college, think about his college fund when he is two. Seventeen might be too late and too expensive.

- If you are in debt, use the snowball method routinely to get out of it. But do not get into debt routinely!

- Calculate your net worth every year just to track your progress. Celebrate if there is a reason for a celebration!

What is richness?

Many people confuse richness and financial security. You should not be one of them. Richness is living a life worth living. Richness is following your passion, loving others and sharing your happiness with others. Richness is about your family, your friends, your purpose. Your legacy.

Of course, it is easier to live a "rich life" if you have some kind of a financial security in place. When you are financially secure, you do not have to stress yourself over one dollar here or there and that is visible. Thus, financial security is only one part of richness, albeit a not too negligible part.

However, richness is not about the latest and newest car brand, the latest and newest clothes, the smart phone that just came out yesterday. Of course, if you can afford them, be my guest; make sure to enjoy these things in life (and believe us when we say that we will do everything in order to help you to make it happen!).

The same goes for financial security. In fact, the people who are financially secure are often kind of invisible. It means that you will not see them parading in the latest clothes just because they can. Financial security is about—surprise—security. It is about the fact that you do not have to worry about tomorrow's food, utilities, the next car payment and your kids' future. Financial security means that you know how money comes in, you know how it goes out, and you are in control. Financial security means that you are the master of your own financial destiny.

Money and self-esteem

The best thing about financial security is that it gives you a boost of self-esteem. Literally. Have you ever met the kind of people that you envied because you were feeling that self-esteem and a sense of security oozed from their pores? I would bet good money on the assumption that they were financially secure people.

Do not be envious. They know nothing special. They only control their finances, and controlling their finances has become their habit. In this book, I show you the exact same method they use. No secrets, no hidden magic formulas, no secret knowledge. It is all laid out in front of you. The only reason why so many people fail to become financially secure is because they fail to make this controlling process their habit.

I will not lie to you, and I will not tell you that it is easy or that you can do it easily, magically, without effort. I am only telling you that if you take responsibility for your finances and do what you have to do, results will inevitably come.

And when you begin to feel the results, you are going to feel the self-esteem boost. You are going to look at the world like if it was a pool of opportunities instead a bunch of constraints. Intellectual prototyping will become a joyful exercise, and your whole life will become a life worth living.

Isn't it what we all yearn for?

In this chapter, you learned:

- Financial security does not just happen. You must be conscious about it.
- Controlling your finances is the only way to get ahead of them. You can do this. You must do this.
- The only one who can make a difference in your finances is you. Nobody is going to save you. You are the master of your financial destiny.
- Tracking and staying below your means can yield things that never would have been possible otherwise.
- Save. Save anything.
- Avoid buying on credit from here on out.

IX. Saving for Retirement

Why should you save money for your retirement?

Imagine that your life is great. You live in financial security, and you have everything you need. And then you turn 60, 62 or 65 and you realize that you will never be able to stop working, that you cannot retire because you have nothing to live by.

Quite a scary prospect, isn't it?

What would you do in such a circumstance?

Work, work and work until you drop dead on the spot? Well, working is a great thing if you do it because you like it. If it is your passion. If you want to create something. If it is about your legacy. We know many people who never stopped working, who in fact worked until their dying day (writers, politicians, businessmen). But come on, that was their personal choice, not a financial constraint!

They worked because they wanted to work, not because they were obligated to and not because they had nothing to live by.

Of course, you do not want to burden your children either. You love them, but you cannot move into their bedrooms, and you cannot be their child. You cannot do that because it is not really moral and because they will not be able to support you. They have themselves to think of, their own mortgage to pay, their children (your grandchildren) to raise, and if they are smart enough, their own retirement to prepare. You cannot force them into a sandwich situation and expect them to help you and their own children while they are trying to prepare for their own old age. (Okay, if your child is Bill Gates, they might be able to help you out, but don't count on that unless you know for sure that your asking for help won't ruin their checking account balance).

You do not really want to depend upon Social Security either. If you are eligible, by all means, go ahead and use your benefits, but please do not consider it as the main paycheck for your retirement period. It will not be enough. You will starve to death more elegantly, but you will still starve to death.

Of course, you can say that you do not intend to live that long. Of course, you can say that you intend to die well before retirement, but— sorry for the dark humor here—what if you stay alive by accident? We have never realized that humans were gods or fortune-tellers. You cannot know how long you will live. And if you live well past your retirement age, what are you going to do then? Who can you count on?

The sad truth is that you have to be prepared for all eventualities. The sad truth is that you have to prepare for retirement upfront, or you will be the guy (or the gal) who does not know what hit them the moment they quit the workforce. If you do not prepare for your retirement, your income will drop dramatically, and your quality of life will go along with it. You will lose that financial and mental self-esteem that you have been so carefully constructing.

So, to sum up, in order to be able to finish this life with dignity, you must prepare for retirement. And you have to do it as soon as possible. In fact, in the case of retirement planning, the mantra "slow and steady wins the race" is truer than ever. If you start your retirement planning early, it will not hurt you; time is the most important factor here. Read this chapter carefully and in detail to understand why.

Now, grab your bound notebook that you used for the intellectual prototyping process and for the measurement of your financial situation. Open a new page and mark "retirement planning." We are going to do a few calculations. Ready?

Okay.

What are the first steps of saving for retirement?

As in every planning operation, before everything else, taking stock is the single most important thing to do. I know that not facing the problem is a nice possibility, and it makes you feel good for now. Avoiding things is usually good in the short term, but it will usually make you feel really, really bad later. So I beg you to do this nasty measurement now. Your future self will thank you.

I suppose that you know what you spend in a month and what you have in terms of savings, because you have previously taken stock and done the exercises. Now, think about your standard of living. If you were to retire now, how much would you need in order to maintain it? It's best to think about it in terms of a single month. Usually, financial consultants say you need 70 percent of your previous income if your salary is high and 90 percent if your salary is lower. When calculating your needs for retirement, your desired monthly income will be somewhere around these figures. (It's easy to understand why you don't need 100 percent; when you retire, you stop saving and instead use the savings you have accumulated.)

When thinking about this, do not lie to yourself. You can lie to anyone else, but never to yourself. If you are the kind of person who likes planning (and I mean, you're really fond of it), do not stop with one single plan. Create a plan A, B, C to cover all possibilities. Let your plan A be your minimum for retirement, covering just your basic needs. Plan B is somewhere in the middle—not a bare minimum but not a dream-like state either. Plan C, have fun with. It's your dream scenario, the one where you take all those trips to Europe and buy that Porsche.

Once that's done, let's take a look at the income that you can count on once you retire. List all the savings, annuities, insurance policies that you have, retirement programs you participate in, and benefits you qualify for. If you can forecast the monthly or annual income that you can expect from these investments and savings, note those figures too. If you plan to work part time at the beginning of your retirement, note those figures as well. The point of this exercise is to know what you currently have and what you can count on later. To be honest, this is very simple; if you know the monthly income that you can count on, you can compare that to your plans A, B and C and design the rest accordingly.

If you have done everything according to this description, by now you have a single number, you know what you have to achieve in terms of monthly income. You have a goal, a calculated and measurable goal.

The next step is to decide when you wish to retire. At the age of 60? 65? It makes all the difference. If you don't yet know, make plans A, B and C for each scenario, first for retirement at 60 and then for retirement at 65. Feel free to play around with this. Remember, it's all about you and your dignity. This is what about makes you happy and secure. Of course, take into account your current health status and life expectancy. (You can use official statistics for this.)

You should now have the following information in your notebook:

Your retirement plans

Your current savings, insurance and retirement policies as well as any benefits you qualify for

The year/age you wish to retire

The monthly income that you need in order to live a life of dignity and happiness, both in terms of dollars and the percentage of your current income (your retirement savings goal)

What if you are young? What if you have nothing in terms of savings?

Dear friend, I don't know you in person. I communicate with you only through the pages of this book. I want to thank you for spending time with me, and I hope that I have been able to help and guide you. The problem is that I don't know your age or your personal situation, so I have to cover all angles. You may be 55, 10 years before retirement, or 20 years old, in college and thinking about financial security for the first time, just looking for the answers. You might have previous savings, but I don't know that for sure. You may have insurance policies. You may not.

I am trying to offer solutions to everyone. As a first example, let me suppose that you have nothing in terms of savings and that you are wet-behind-the-ears young, just out of high school. In this "simple" case, there is only one figure you have to keep in mind. If you do not take into account future inflation, if instead you only think about the sum that you will need once you retire, financial planners usually say that you need 150 times (!) your current monthly income in order to maintain your current standard of living.

Let's assume that you earn $4000 per month, and you spend everything at once. (I strongly hope you don't though.) In that case, you will need

$$150 * 4000 \text{ USD} = 600,000 \text{ USD}$$

Yes, you read that correctly; you will need six hundred thousand dollars in retirement funds, savings, etc. for you to be able to maintain your current living standard. That probably sounds like an astonishingly huge amount to you right now. But it really isn't. Why? Because the key is long term, and the operative word is "interest." In the case of loans and mortgages, interest works against you. In the case of savings, interest works for you.

Age Started to Save	Monthly Savings		No. of Years to Save	Retirement Savings to Achive	
	assuming interest rate is 6.5%	assuming interest rate is 3.5%		assuming interest rate is 6.5%	assuming interest rate is 3.5%
less than 40 year old	$280	$580	40	$600,000	$600,000
40 years old	$1,270	$830	25	$600,000	$600,000
55 years old	$3,600	$4, 000	10	$600,000	$573,000

Let's do a quick calculation with the bankrate.com calculator. Say you deposit $1 initially and then $280 every month. That is not even 10 percent of your monthly income, so you shouldn't even feel it. (If you are so stretched that you do feel it, you are doing something wrong. Please review the debt chapter immediately.) Usually it is recommended that you save 10 percent of your income throughout your career for retirement, but right now let's simply calculate with $280 because that will give you the $600,000 you need at the end of a 40-year savings period (supposing a 6.5 percent interest rate; if the interest rate is down to 3.5, you need to deposit $580).

It is fairly simple and straightforward. Let's suppose another example. You're 40 years old and you also earn $4,000, but you have nothing in terms of retirement savings. You want to start now. As such, you do not have the whole 40 years to assemble those investments, so you will have to go much more quickly. You will have to save much more each month. In this case if you want the same $600,000 in time to retire, you need to sock away $1270 each month if the interest rate is 3.5 and $830 if it's 6.5.

Scared yet? Let's do another calculation. If you wake up at the age of 55, giving you a 10-year savings period, you will have to deposit a whopping $3,600 per month in order to achieve the same $600,000 result. That's essentially your entire income. And that's supposing a 6.5 percent interest rate. If you deposit all $4,000 each month with a 3.5 percent interest rate, you won't even make it to $600,000. You'll come in at $572,000 at the end of 10 years.

The implications

So what does it all mean? It means that if you do not start saving early, or if you have done nothing in terms of retirement planning up until now, you can almost be sure about the fact that your living standards will dramatically fall once you retire. Sadly, the older you are, the worse your situation is. However, let me tell you that there is no such thing as "There is no point in starting now." It's possible that you are now 55, and you can be sure that you won't be able to maintain your $4,000 per month lifestyle. It is possible that you will have to make due with $2,000 instead. But $2,000 is still better than nothing. So do yourself (your current version and your old age one) a favor and start planning for retirement now. Remember: slow and steady wins the race. If interest can work for you during a 10-year-long period, it's still better than nothing. It is never too late.

If you are 20 and wet behind the ears, you're obviously not too late. But the numbers I presented above should convince you that you should start planning your retirement now. In this case, pacing yourself is truer than ever. If you begin to save for retirement now, money and interest will work for you during the whole 40-year-long savings period. And that is a great thing too.

Now let's take a quick break. Go on and play with the savings calculator a bit; it will give you a fair idea of what you need to do in the future.

Be a responsible adult

Are you back? Great. Did you do your calculations? Even better. Do you have the numbers in your bound notebook? I hope so, because you need them now. The last part of the financial discussion should have convinced you that you need to plan your retirement. Or, more accurately, you need to plan your retirement as soon as possible. Like right now.

If you are in your early 20s, start right now. If you are in your early 30s, start right now. If you are in your 40s, start right now. If you are in your 50s, start right now. What are you waiting for?!

I know that you can always find shabby excuses to not save for retirement. "I'm still young. I have my student loans to pay. I have a mortgage. I have my kids to educate." Stop. Just stop it. That is not the way to go. Hell to the no. Forget those lame excuses and start acting like a responsible adult. If you cannot save for retirement, it means that you live above your means or that you are up to your neck in debt. If that is the case, run back to the debt chapter and start doing those exercises. (That's if you haven't started doing them yet. If you did, kudos. You made the first and most important step towards financial security, both for now and in the future.)

One more thing: your retirement savings are not to be used in case of an emergency. Other than the fact that breaking up your retirement savings early is often heavily taxed and penalized, the goal of your retirement fund is to fund your retirement. Got it? No touching. Later on we will create an emergency fund, so don't worry about that now. Just remember that your retirement fund is just that: your retirement fund. Circulate, people; there is nothing to see here!

The golden rule of retirement savings

Long term matters. (Do I really have to say "slow and steady wins the race" again?) 40 years of patient saving might give you incredible results, sums that you've never heard of much less held in your hand. If you start your savings early enough, interest works for you instead of against you. (And this is the main reason why you should save upfront for huge spending; never take out a loan.) Because of this simple truth, wherever you are, irrespective of age, you should start saving for retirement. The sooner the better.

Now let's take a look at the practical part.

Here is what you can and should do, in this order:

The planning phase

- If you haven't done it yet, calculate your needs (the monthly income that you wish to receive, then the aggregated amount of money that you will need once you retire). Do not forget the 150x rule.

- According to your needs, create your retirement plans A, B and C. Of course, you should aim for C. You deserve it!

- Take a look at your current savings, policies and the benefits you qualify for. It is okay to ask around, and it is okay to check on contracts, interest rates and so on. Make sure that you have all of the information you need.

- Calculate the money that you still have to save while you are still active (subtract your current savings from the dream figure, and do it for all three of your retirement plans).

- Use the savings calculator just to have an inkling as to what you need to do in order to have that money when you retire.

- If you want to do all of the math with the help of a calculator, I suggest that you use the CNN Money retirement calculator. This is a great tool that takes into account all the factors that I discussed above, and it will give you the information you need, down to the monthly savings that you have to produce in order to survive later.

The action phase

- If your employer offers a 401(k), make sure to contribute to it. First of all, if you use a 401(k), you can benefit from tax deduction, which means less taxable income for you. Secondly, employees also receive a contribution from the company in question in most cases (called a "matching contribution"), which might be as high as 50%. Do not let that free money pass you by! Thirdly, this income is not called tax-deferred income for nothing; in fact, you do not pay the taxes when you retire and withdraw the money. It simply means that, as this account is not taxed every year, more money works for you instead of the state. Of course, if you use this account/amount before retirement, you are heavily taxed and penalized so make sure to avoid it. That is why we will be creating an emergency fund later. One more thing—if your employer has another pension plan, make sure to contribute to it. If your employer does not offer such a plan, go ahead and lobby for it. Even the Department of Labor suggests that employees ask for it, as it might be beneficial for everyone. Do not hesitate!

- Secondly, find a good IRA (individual retirement account). These are, in fact, simple retirement savings accounts offered by financial institutions acting on the market. In certain cases, you can also benefit from tax breaks and taxed deference with IRAs too, so it is a good thing to look around and find one that is good for you. Just for your information, when you take a look at the market, you will be offered three main types of IRAs: the traditional IRA (tax deductible scheme, with a tax-advantaged growth), the Roth IRA (savings are paid by money after tax, but growth and even withdrawals might be tax free) and finally the Rollover IRA (money coming from an employer's retirement plan, a 401(k) for instance). This latter is especially interesting if you plan to switch workplaces. Later on, you can convert your IRA to a Roth IRA. The Internet is all over with providers who offer such services and advice on that issue. This is not the place to discuss it in length; it's more something you do in person. In fact, I recommend that you make sure to consult your financial consultant so that you are not overtaxed and do not lose your savings.

- If you have created a 6-month security buffer, you can think about investing and saving more money. In a later chapter, I will advise you concerning investment issues.

- Just a word of caution though: make sure that you distribute your assets between different investments and savings. The 2008 crisis made many employees lose their whole retirement savings because they did not pay attention to this simple truth. Do not be one of these people! You never know when another crisis might strike. There is no systemic security in a capitalist system; you have to create your own. So repeat after me, slowly and patiently, "Asset allocation and distribution."

- For instance, stocks are designed for long-term investment. Not for two months and not for two years. You will not get rich like that, much less secure. A short crisis might even kill the lion's share of that wealth, but growth might build it back slowly. So stocks are really for the long term. And I would not think about stocks as stocks; instead, think about them as businesses and invest in businesses instead of stocks. Finally, make sure to gradually shift toward bonds as you grow old. Yes, consult a financial wizard concerning this issue too.

- Lastly, at least know about the potential Social Security benefits that you qualify for (if you do). However, do not really count on it. You are the only one you can count on, right? If you do not know whether you qualify, visit the Social Security estimator.

When retired

- Even when you retire, you have to continue to be cautious about your finances. Yes, you will have to control your spending and track your income, just like you have had to do your whole life. Financial security is all about continuous control. You cannot give up this control when you retire. Stick to the habits until your dying day.

- As a second step, take a look around your financial kingdom. Calculate the price of withdrawal in the case of your savings.

Always take out more of the less tax-advantaged savings, and let your taxable savings live a little shorter than your tax-advantaged savings. But, on the other hand, do not forget the principle of asset allocation. Do not withdraw your whole savings at once, and make sure that you continue to have multiple sources of income.

- Think about taking out a reverse mortgage. It is not subject to income tax payment, but it is a complex and dangerous financial instrument, so make sure that you understand what you are stepping into.

- Think about working! Now that you have finished the intellectual prototyping process, you know what your passion is, and why would you want to stop working on your passion? And why would you not let your tax-deferred money grow stronger?

- Lastly, if you really are retired, or if you cannot work anymore, think about moving somewhere that prices are lower and you have to spend less.

If you really pay attention beforehand, retirement might be a beautiful phase of your life: children, grandchildren, doing what you always wanted to do. Personal freedom. Find it all in financial security! Financial security doesn't come from nowhere; you have to work for it. And you have to work for it right now. In the case of retirement planning, slow and steady wins this race and next year's race too. Start now. No time to lose!

In this chapter, you learned:

- When it comes to saving for retirement, the best time to start is yesterday. The second best time is right now.

- A good rule of thumb is that you need 150x what you make now to compensate for inflation when you retire.

- Have 3 plans for retirement: good, better, and best. Aim for best.

dignissim deterruisset at, nec graece consequat in. Vim at liber imperdiet assueverit. Pro no putent facete, eu aperiri consequuntur voluptatibus quo. Eirmod aperiam sed et. Omittam gubergren ad duo, ipsum accusamus quo an, cu brute fuisset noluisse eos.

Vix harum dolorum partiendo te, vim at alia legendas. Mel ut tamquam nusquam sensibus, labores volutpat salutandi sed an. Ea mei facer tantas erroribus, et natum melius vim, enim dicat mentitum eum et. His eu quem audiam, unum primis sed cu. Est ei

X. Wills, Trusts and Estate Planning

In this chapter, you will learn about wills, and you will put into place your own will and set up a personal or family trust.

We all die sometime, and we want our wealth to go to our loved ones or to people we choose—not to the government! You want your will and trust to be legally valid and uncontestable so they pass automatically to your designated beneficiaries.

Start your prototyping by taking the time now to go on the Internet, putting in search terms such as "preparing a will" or "preparing a trust," and glance through the results. What are you seeing? What are the commonalities? What is the advice given? How much will it cost? Can you do it yourself? What do you think, how hard

"The glass is half full"

—*Optimist*

"The glass is half empty"

—*Pessimist*

"The IRS took half because you didn't plan"

—*Estate Planning Attorney*

does it appear? Take good notes; be sure to record where you find good information so you can return later to read again and read more. Change your source by visiting a bookstore or library and just browse to see how that information "squares" with what you learned online. Keep looking, keep thinking, and keep taking notes. (You've got your bound notebook, right?) Talk to your friends and neighbors to try out your ideas and the ways you feel are best to go about putting a will and trust in place right now. Build a great "prototype" plan of what seems to make the most sense as you prepare to take action—and you will need to take action, if you don't want to end up like the cartoon above from Stu's Views.

Make the subject your own. Work long enough and think deeply enough that the subject loses any mystery or complexity that you may have thought and becomes "ho hum, pass the bread and butter" sort of, "I can handle this! What's so hard about this?" Again, the need for a will and for a trust is simple—as you prepare yourself for prosperity and financial security, you need to protect what you save and invest. A will makes sure your wealth goes to those you want to benefit rather than to the government. A trust does the same thing. These are wealth protection tools at the heart of preparing to be prosperous and financially secure, not just today but into the future for you and for those you love.

As you do your Internet, library, and friend searches for your prototyping and other exercises, use the following information (representative and as good as any) for comparison/contrast and understanding of how you want to move forward.

You will see quickly that there are legal forms online that you can either download or purchase so you can do your will and trust yourself. If you feel, after you have done your best and after you have spent the time prototyping and note taking, that you want an attorney to look over what you have done and "bless" it or give advice, that is your choice.

"Last Wills & Trusts Questions" by A.L. Kennedy, Demand Media http://info.legalzoom.com/last-wills-trusts-questions-4140.html

"Last wills and trusts are two ways to pass your property to your chosen beneficiaries after your death. Last wills and trusts can be used separately or together. Answering some basic questions about last wills and trusts can help you understand what kind of estate planning is best for you and your family. Although an attorney's help is not required to create a valid will or trust, it is wise to consult an attorney when doing your estate planning.

What Are Wills and Trusts?

Both a will and a trust are mechanisms by which you can pass your property to the persons of your choice after you die. A will is a written document that governs how and to whom your property should be distributed after you die. A trust, on the other hand, is a legal arrangement where one person, the trustee, manages property for the benefit of another person, the beneficiary.

What Happens if I Die Without a Will or Trust? If you die without leaving a valid will or trust, you are said to have died intestate. When a person dies intestate, the state's inheritance laws govern how that person's property is distributed. In most states, your spouse and children would receive your property if you died intestate. If you have no spouse or children, your parents or siblings may inherit your property. If there is no one who is qualified to inherit your property under state law, then the state takes your property.

What Are the Benefits and Disadvantages of a Will? The benefit of wills is that they are usually very flexible, according to attorney Dianne Reis. As long as your will meets the state's basic rules for making a valid will, the state will usually uphold your wishes as stated in the will, no matter what they are. The major disadvantage to a will is that it does not cover all of your assets. Joint bank accounts, jointly-owned property, insurance policies and some other assets have their own rules for passing to one person when another dies. These are known as "nonprobate" assets, because the probate court, which governs the execution of a will, has no power over these assets.

What Are the Benefits and Disadvantages of a Trust? A trust allows you to pass some or all of your assets to your chosen beneficiaries without having to deal with the probate court. Because your assets pass to the trust's beneficiaries immediately upon your death, the probate court's intervention is not required. One disadvantage to trusts, however, is that they can be difficult to set up properly, and some of your property may have to be titled in the name of the trust in order for your beneficiaries to receive it when you die.

How Do a Will and Trust Work Together? Using a trust in combination with a will is one way to avoid the disadvantage of having to probate the will and the disadvantage of having to title assets in the name of the trust. In these situations, the trust is created but is left "unfunded," or without holding any assets. The will, known as a "pour-over will," leaves all of your assets to the trust, which then distributes them to your beneficiaries."

Wealth accumulation is about both wealth creation and wealth preservation. If you spend $1.22 for every dollar you earn, you'll always be broke, whether you're making $50,000 a year or $5 million a year. Wealth creation focuses on increasing your family's income while managing cost and accumulating assets, which may take time. However, your wealth preservation plans need to be put into action right now. If you fail to put your wealth preservation and financial defenses in place, you could lose everything you have worked for within seconds.

How is this possible? It's easy. Unexpected and untimely life events are the single most impactful destroyer of wealth creation. Life events are neither trivial nor avoidable; they are in fact, inevitable. Life events are the single most impactful and devastating effect to families and their wealth creation. Families can take years or decades to accumulate assets, only to watch them destroyed or depleted in an instant due to the lack of preparation for a life event that was sure to come.

The most important part of your financial future is how well you prepare yourself for life's inevitabilities.

X. Wills, Trusts and Estate Planning

Planning for death and disability may not be popular and can feel downright morbid, but these are the life's inevitabilities that we are all going to face someday. The success of your family finances depends on how well prepared you are to face the challenges of life. A living will and trust represents the first building block in the protection principles because getting your health care wishes and selecting a health care agent doesn't cost much money and can have a profound impact on you and your family when that fateful day comes. Go online and learn as much as you can about how to set up a living will. You owe it to your family.

What happens if you don't have a will or living trust when you die? If you do not specify through a valid will or living trust who will receive your property, state law controls and distributes your property to your spouse and/or your closest heirs, which may or may not be what you want. Furthermore, if you fail to nominate a guardian for your minor children, the state could appoint someone you don't trust as the legal guardian of your children. Finally, by failing to appoint someone to carry out your wishes, the state can appoint anyone as the administrator of your property, and the administrator may have to pay certain fees or post a bond at the expense of your estate before he or she can begin to distribute your assets.

Whatever amount of money and assets you've accumulated through your entire life, the government can decide how to divide your entire estate completely against your wishes, which is why you must create or update your living will or trust.

In this chapter, you learned:

- While you're alive, you must determine where you want your money to go in your passing.
- Nobody wants to admit that they're mortal, and discussing a will can be morbid. But it's one of the best ways to take care of what you've built after you're gone.
- If you die without leaving behind a will, someone else gets to decide what happens to your assets.

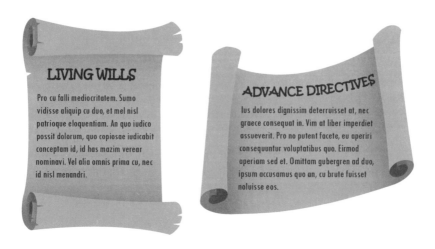

LIVING WILLS

Pro cu falli mediocritatem. Sumo vidisse aliquip cu duo, et mel nisl patrioque eloquentiam. An quo iudico possit dolorum, quo copiosae iudicabit conceptam id, id has mazim verear nominavi. Vel alia omnis prima cu, nec id nisl menandri.

ADVANCE DIRECTIVES

Ius dolores dignissim deterruisset at, nec graece consequat in. Vim at liber imperdiet assueverit. Pro no putent facete, eu aperiri consequuntur voluptatibus quo. Eirmod aperiam sed et. Omittam gubergren ad duo, ipsum accusamus quo an, cu brute fuisset noluisse eos.

XI. Living Wills and Advance Directives

A living will is a legal document that defines your wishes regarding life prolonging medical treatments. These instructions are also called an advance directive, health care directive, or a physician's directive. Essentially, a living will acts as your voice that specifies which treatments you do or do not want applied to you in the event you either suffer from a terminal illness or are in a permanent vegetative state.

A living will does not become effective unless you are incapacitated, which usually requires certification from your doctor and another doctor who both agree that you are either suffering from a terminal illness or permanently unconscious. If you suffer a heart attack, but do not become permanently unconscious, a living will does not have any effect. You would still be resuscitated, even if you had a living will indicating that you don't want life-prolonging procedures. A living will only goes into effect when two doctors agree that your ultimate recovery is hopeless.

Advance directives are your written instructions that define your medical care preferences, which your family and doctors must legally consult if you're unable to make your own health care decisions. Having written instructions can reduce confusion or disagreement among your family members.

Without such written instructions, family members are left to decide what medical treatments they believe you should have; nobody will know what you would decide for yourself. Unless all family members can agree, the resulting confusion and arguing can tear a family apart.

Several years back, a close friend of mine went out with some coworkers for drinks. After the group split up for the evening, my friend and his buddy went back to their house to continue drinking and socializing.

Being in an inebriated state of mind, they thought it would be cool to check out his friend's gun collection. In this state of mind sometimes people make stupid decisions. They both came up with the idea that it might be funny to put what they thought was an empty and unloaded gun against the side of their head and wonder what it would be like to play Russian Roulette. What they thought was a harmless, unloaded handgun turned out to be otherwise. In a split second and one fatally bad lapse in judgment, my friend put the pistol to his head, pulled the trigger, and shot himself by mistake.

Miraculously, he survived for a short period of time, but fell into a coma with no chance of ever regaining consciousness or the life he once knew. On life support in the hospital, my friend's family members were not only grieving over the accident, but now they had the burden of deciding whether to leave him on life support or pull him off it. Because he had not created a living will, his wishes in that situation were completely unknown.

Now you have one group of family members who want to keep him alive on life support indefinitely and another group of family members who want to take him off life support so he can rest in peace. Yet nobody knew what they should do because the person who should have made that decision for himself was incapacitated.

Ultimately, the family members agreed to make the difficult decision to pull my friend off life support. If they hadn't come to an agreement as a family, they could have potentially dragged their argument through the courts, which would have prolonged the family disagreement and possibly damaged relationships between family members forever.

Yet this could have all been avoided had my friend just taken the simple step of creating a living will to state his intentions if he were ever physically incapacitated.

To get true peace of mind, you need to plan for the possibility that you may become incapacitated. As unpleasant as this thought may be, what's even more unpleasant is the thought that if you had just taken the time to create a living will, you could avoid leaving behind emotional wreckage for your loved ones to clean up.

Imagine the emotional turmoil that could ensue if a mother wants to keep her baby alive on life support indefinitely, but a father wants his child to pass away peacefully. What might happen if a husband or wife wishes for his or her spouse to be pulled off life support, but the parents believe that their child should stay on life support for as long as possible? Can you see how such emotional dilemmas could shred relationships irreparably?

Don't just make a living will for yourself, but for your parents, your spouse, and your children, not to mention your relatives. Don't leave life and death decisions to chance.

What kind of medical treatments do you want?

In some states, living wills may be called health care declarations or health care directives. The main directive of your living is to define the types of medical treatments and life-sustaining measures you do and don't want, such as mechanical breathing (respiration and ventilation), tube feeding or resuscitation.

In determining your wishes, think about your values and what you feel would make your life not worth living. Would you want treatments to extend your life in any situation? Would you want treatment only if there's a possibility of complete recovery? Would you want treatment to ease pain and discomfort if you were terminally ill?

Although you can't predict every possible medical situation that could arise, consider the following common types of situations and talk to your doctor if you have any questions:

Resuscitation: Restarts the heart when it has stopped beating (cardiac death). Determine if and when you would want to be resuscitated by cardiopulmonary resuscitation (CPR) or by a device that delivers an electric shock to stimulate the heart.

Mechanical ventilation: Takes over your breathing if you're unable to do so. Consider if, when and for how long you would want to be placed on a mechanical ventilator.

Nutritional and hydration assistance: Supplies the body with nutrients and fluids intravenously or via a tube in the stomach. Decide if, when and for how long you would want to be fed in this manner.

Dialysis: Removes waste from your blood and manages fluid levels if your kidneys no longer function. Determine if, when and for how long you would want to receive this treatment.

Besides specifying medical treatments you may or may not want, you may also want to specify if you wish to donate organs for transplants or donate your entire body for scientific study. If you wish to donate your body for scientific study, contact the nearest medical school to your home for more details.

Who do you want to make decisions for you?

A second advance directive is called a medical power of attorney (POA), which legally designates a specific individual—referred to as your health care agent or proxy—to make medical decisions for you in the event that you're unable to do so. A medical POA is sometimes called a durable power of attorney for health care. However, it is different from a power of attorney authorizing someone to make financial transactions for you.

While your living will can state what type of medical treatments you do or do not want, there will be medical situations that your living will will not cover. In that event, the decision falls on your designated health care agent (who has medical power of attorney), who you trust will make decisions for you. This person will be guided by your living will but has the authority to interpret your wishes in situations that aren't specifically described in your living will. A health care agent can be especially useful if your family is opposed to some of your wishes or is divided about them. No matter what your family members may want, your health care agent has final control over all your medical issues.

For your health care agent, choose someone that you trust will have your interests at heart and is willing to act according to your wishes. Your health care agent doesn't necessarily have to be a family member and may not even live in the same city or state as you do.

I know that injury, illness and death aren't easy subjects to talk about, but by planning ahead you can ensure that you receive the type of medical care you want while taking the burden off your family from guessing and arguing what you might want done. Start by talking with your loved ones; let them know about your advance directives, and explain your feelings about medical care and what you'd want done in specific instances.

Explain to your loved ones why these advance directives are important to you. Treat this subject in a matter-of-fact and reassuring manner. For peace of mind, you have to prepare for the inevitable.

In this chapter, you learned:

- Accidents happen. If one happens to you, you want your family to know how you'd like it handled.

- Leave someone you trust in charge to make decisions in the event that you are unable to do so.

XII. Establish a Living Trust

While a living will defines your wishes in the event you are incapacitated and unable to make medical decisions for yourself, a living trust defines how to distribute your assets in the event of your death.

An ordinary trust designates someone to manage or take care of property for someone else's benefit, but a living trust goes into effect while you are still alive. A living trust transfers title to your property from your name to that of the trustee of the living trust. You can use the trust to gather your property under one document so that it is distributed efficiently after your death.

When you put your property into a trust, the trustee of that trust owns the property; you are no longer the legal owner of the transferred property. This doesn't mean you have no control of your assets. Since you will likely be your trust's initial trustee, you will still be in charge of your property. You can do whatever you want with it. You can leave it alone, take it out of the trust, or use it as you had been before the trust was created. A living trust is an easy way to organize your assets and manage them as a single unit.

Everyone needs a will, but not everyone needs a trust. While living trusts are an excellent way to avoid probate, do you really need one?

I didn't set up my family trust until I was the owner of a very large business and had many personal assets that I didn't want to get caught up in Probate. Probate is the legal process that distributes a person's property after death. The main reason to avoid probate is because it takes time and incurs probate charges. Would you rather have your money go to a designated charity or relative, or to the government for their role in distributing your assets in ways that may not be what you wish?

There are a growing number of ways to transfer assets to inheritors free of probate within weeks or, at most, months of death. These include making gifts before death, adding a pay-on-death designation to a bank account, holding your house in joint tenancy with right of survivorship with your spouse or partner, and naming a beneficiary for life insurance and retirement accounts.

But only the living trust can be used for all types of property and offers the broad planning flexibility of a will. With a living trust, you can name alternate beneficiaries to inherit property if your primary beneficiary dies before you do. That's something you can't accomplish with joint tenancy or a pay-on-death bank account.

One drawback of a living trust is that living trusts are considerably more time-consuming to establish, involve more ongoing maintenance, and are more trouble to modify than a regular will. A lawyer-drafted trust will cost upwards of $1,000, though the cost will shrink dramatically if you use a self-help tool to make your own trust.

To decide if you need a living trust, consider these factors:

- How old are you? Living trusts often do not make sense for middle-income people in decent health who are under the age of 55 or 60. Remember, a living trust does nothing for you during your life. In the meantime, a serviceable will, which is easier to establish, will do a fine job of transferring your property to your loved ones in the highly unlikely event that you die without warning.

- Another reason why it makes little sense for a healthy younger person of moderate means to worry about probate avoidance is that the problem may go away. In just the last ten years, easy-to-use probate-avoidance techniques, such as being able to name a beneficiary to inherit securities free of probate, have gained wide acceptance. This trend will probably continue.

- How rich are you? After age, the second biggest factor in deciding whether or not to create a living trust is wealth. At the risk of oversimplifying, the wealthier you are, the more you can save for your inheritors by avoiding probate. For example, a 45-year-old with $10 million might decide that it's not too soon to think about probate avoidance. However, another 45-year-old with $300,000 might sensibly decide to wait many years before making a trust.

- What kinds of assets you own is a significant factor, too. Owning a small business, rental property, or other significant assets that you don't want tied up during probate might push you to create a living trust at a younger age. Even if there's only a small chance that you'll die soon, you don't want to risk making your executor report to a judge for a year or more if you die unexpectedly.

- Are you married? If you are married, and you and your spouse plan to leave the bulk of your property to one another, there is less reason to obsess about avoiding probate at an early age. If, like many couples, you own your major assets together, probate won't be necessary for those assets. Most states let surviving spouses use expedited probate procedures that are faster and cheaper than standard probate.

Death is inevitable. You must plan ahead and decide who you want controlling your medical decisions and financial assets: the state or someone you love and trust? Death and disability can come at any time so you need to be prepared now.

The three basic questions you need to ask yourself involve children, money, and medical. Who gets custody of your children in the event you pass away? Who gets your financial assets? What kind of medical treatments do you wish if you are unable to make your own decisions? By answering those three questions ahead of time, you'll make your passing away less of a burden for your loved ones, siblings, children, and family members.

So, your task now is to prepare your will and your trust and get them made "legal" as needed. Get it done now, and get them into a safe place.

You can do it! You know about wills and trusts now better than anyone around you or any who profess to specialize in these things. Your notebook is filled with sources, ideas, facts, locations of documents and forms, people you've talked to, legal worries that you need to consider, etc. Just put these documents into place and put them in your safe place (fireproof and waterproof and easily transportable in case of disaster or emergency).

In this chapter, you learned:
- A living trust determines how you'd like your assets distributed in the event of your death.
- Not everyone needs a living trust. A living trust is best utilized by people over the age of 55.
- The three biggest questions that should be considered when it comes to living wills are regarding your children, your money, and your medical treatment.

XIII. Secure Adequate Life Insurance

"Because term life insurance is a pure death benefit, its primary use is to provide coverage of financial responsibilities, for the insured. Such responsibilities may include, but are not limited to, consumer debt, dependent care, college education for dependents, funeral costs, and mortgages. Term life insurance is generally chosen in favor of permanent life insurance because it is usually much less expensive (depending on the length of the term). Many financial advisors or other experts commonly recommend term life insurance as a means to cover potential expenses until such time that there are sufficient funds available from savings to protect those whom the insurance coverage was intended to protect."
(http://en.wikipedia.org/wiki/Term_life_insurance)

In this chapter, you will learn about life insurance, and you will put into place your own basic policies to protect your family.

"Do I have to have life insurance?" "Yes!" is the answer.

Get out your prototyping notebook and get after these "cattle" and get them chased down and into your truck. Start online, go to the library, gather your notes, think about it, prototype a plan, talk to your friends and family, and form in your mind and in your notebook how you are going to go about satisfying this requirement for prosperity and financial security. What about term or whole life insurance? How much do I need? For how long should I set as the term? Which companies are best? How do I go about buying an insurance policy? You now are in search of answers on your own to these and other questions. There is plenty of good information out there as long as you are "prototyping" and not believing in anything until you have seen enough and thought enough to understand what is going on. Stay away from life insurance sales people until you understand what is going on and have an opinion about your needs. When you decide to buy, get at least three valid and reputable bids from people you trust. The shysters are a dime a dozen in this and the used car businesses, so be wise.

Life insurance: why you need it

So, another action to take right now is to get adequate life insurance. You need to guard your income and assets from life's inevitable and unavoidable events such as death, disability, or job loss.

From experience watching families after they've suffered a devastating financial life event, such as the death of the major income provider, I want you to be prepared as part of your building for prosperity and financial security.

The cycle of life is ever present, and there is nothing you can do to prevent your passing in time. The decision is solely yours on how that passing will affect your family emotionally and financially. It can be hard enough to deal emotionally with the loss of a loved one, but I have seen first-hand the devastation from the untimely passing of a primary breadwinner and its catastrophic impact on the family financially. Please take warning: Nothing is worse than to see a family struggle to maintain their sanity and family bond when faced with the possibility of losing everything they have known. If you get anything out of this book at all, I hope you understand the importance of protecting your family for life's inevitabilities.

Most people think of life insurance as something only rich people need. They think of life insurance only when a rich, old uncle dies and leaves them with a lot of money, like winning the lottery. Life insurance isn't just for certain people but for everybody. Think of life insurance as both inevitable life event protection and income replacement insurance.

It is never a matter of if, but when, a disruptive life event will happen to you. Unfortunately, most people only think about inevitable life events like death only after it has already occurred, which means that most people are least prepared emotionally and financially. You can never control when you might have an "untimely passing," but you can control its impact on your loved ones.

My first question to anyone is, "Do you have life insurance?"

When a person dies, you've lost all the income they could have made for all those remaining years. You can't replace that lost person, but you can replace that lost income through life insurance.

So when I asked my friend, "Do you have life insurance?" can you guess the worst possible answer he could give me? As soon as he told me that he didn't have life insurance, I knew there was nothing I could do for him other than paying for the wake.

The first step in protecting your family is understanding the necessity and importance for life insurance no matter what your income level may be. Life insurance is basically a financial instrument that allows you to protect your family and loved ones when you're gone.

Life insurance is a major component of your financial foundation because it covers all of your short and long-term un-funded liabilities as well as replacing your family's loss of your income.

Consider the following example:

John and Mary Sue are a typical family, living the American Dream. They own a beautiful home and are raising two children (ages 5 and 7). John has a promising career making a six-figure income per year while Mary Sue is a stay-at-home mom. On the surface, they appear wealthy, happy, and successful.

As long as nothing happens, their lives would remain secure, but what would happen to this family if John were to suddenly die in a car accident or from an incurable disease? First, John provides the family's sole source of income, and if he dies, Mary Sue no longer has his income to make the house payment, car payments, or feed and clothe the family. Without John's income to pay for the house and cars, how can Mary Sue possibly pay for these un-funded liabilities, especially a mortgage that may require another twenty years of payments?

Second, John and Mary Sue have two kids that will need care for years until they are able to take care of themselves. Where will the money come from just to pay their normal living expenses? What if these children want to go to college? With John's income gone, who is going to fund their long-term college expenses?

Without life insurance, Mary Sue won't be able to make the house payments, which means she'll lose the house to foreclosure and be forced to move into a smaller place in a more affordable part of town. If there are car payments remaining, Mary Sue may lose the cars as well.

Without John's income, Mary Sue will have to drastically cut back on her family's lifestyle, find a way to earn some sort of income to pay for daily expenses such as food and shelter, all while going through the emotionally painful process of grieving for John's death, which has taken away her husband and the father of her children. Mary Sue has no choice but to survive financially, but how much added emotional stress will that put on her and the children?

John and Mary Sue's story is one that I see played out often.

All of these problems could have been avoided if John and Mary Sue would have gotten adequate life insurance coverage. Let's look at how life insurance could protect John and Mary Sue in the event of his death.

Consideration #1: Income Replacement

Suppose John's income is $120,000 per year. The immediate consequence of John's death would be the loss of his income. Without any income at all, how could Mary Sue pay her monthly bills such as utilities or groceries, not to mention larger expenses such as car or mortgage payments?

As a form of income replacement, life insurance can provide immediate financial relief. Given the young age of their children, Mary Sue will likely need to provide for her children for at least ten more years, so John's life insurance should replace at least 10 years' worth of income so Mary Sue could continue to stay home and raise the children.

Consideration #2: Mortgage

Let's assume that John and Mary Sue own a house with a mortgage balance of $350,000 that has a 30-year fixed mortgage with 25 more years remaining. If John should die, how can Mary Sue possibly afford to continue making mortgage payments, especially when the obligations of mortgage payments are supported with John's six-figure income as the primary means of payback?

Can Mary Sue, a stay-at-home mother, suddenly get a job that's close to replacing John's income so she can afford to make her monthly mortgage payments? Maybe, but can she do it within the next 30 days before the next mortgage payment is due? Depending on how long Mary Sue has been out of the work force, how easy will it be for her to get a job, let alone one that can match John's previous six-figure income and do it all within the next 30 days?

After taxes, housing is a family's single largest liability. Life insurance needs to cover the costs of the home because the home is the hub of the family, and in times of grieving, the home is the only place that provides safety and certainty, especially to young children.

Can you imagine the trauma that many families experience when the primary breadwinner passes away and the surviving spouse and children can no longer afford to live in their own house? Not only do these survivors have to deal with the emotional grief of losing a parent and spouse, but they also have the financial stress of losing their home and moving to an unfamiliar, more affordable neighborhood that will likely be far from their friends.

Consideration #3: Debt

Besides a mortgage, most families also have numerous other debts such as car payments and credit card debt. Eliminate John's income and how will Mary Sue afford such recurring debt payments as a car loan in addition to all her other expenses that were completely affordable when John's income arrived regularly every month?

Let's assume that John and Mary Sue have minimal debt amounting to roughly $50,000 to pay off two car payments and any credit card debt. Families should get enough life insurance to cover these liabilities so there will be one less expense in the household to worry about.

Consideration #4: College Tuition

Parents such as John and Mary Sue might have planned for their children to attend college when they're older. So not only will Mary Sue have expenses in raising her two children, but she'll also have to save money for college tuition for the two of them.

Assuming the average tuition for a four-year degree would be $120,000, Mary Sue now has to make a difficult choice. Can she afford to send her children to college? With two children reaching college age in a little over ten years, the prospect of college tuition represents another liability that Mary Sue must face.

The market perception of insurance is one of hitting the lottery, but as you can see it is not the case. It is however the most important financial tool you can have to protect your family.

Knowing that John and Mary Sue need life insurance to replace John's income in the event of an untimely passing to pay off their mortgage, pay off transportation and credit card liabilities, and fully fund the children's college savings accounts so Mary Sue can send her two children to college, this is approximately what John and Mary Sue need for adequate life insurance coverage:

Income Replacement for ten years at $120,000 = $1,200,000

Mortgage - $350,000

Debt - $50,000

College Tuition - $240,000

Grand Total coverage needed to feel safe and secure = $1,840,000

Since John and Mary Sue are relatively young and in great health, insurance coverage in this amount is relatively inexpensive with monthly or quarterly payments that can easily fit into their household budget.

Besides getting a life insurance policy for John, the couple should also get a smaller life insurance policy for Mary Sue. Even though Mary Sue doesn't provide any income, she offsets certain expenses by staying home and taking care of the kids. If she should die, John would need to pay child care expenses for someone to watch over his children while he works.

Mary Sue's life insurance policy doesn't need to be as great as John's policy, but it should cover the expenses needed to replace Mary Sue because John will be unable to do certain things for himself. In this case, Mary Sue might only need a $250,000 life insurance policy to pay for child care expenses over the next ten years.

One key with life insurance is that you never need the same amount of insurance coverage throughout your entire life. For example, when you're young and single, your expenses and liabilities are likely low, plus you probably won't have someone depending on your income for survival. In that situation, you may not need life insurance at all.

When you get married, you now have a spouse who depends on you, if not financially, then emotionally. At the very least, life insurance can cover basic burial and funeral expenses. However, if one spouse is the primary breadwinner, then life insurance should be used for income replacement for the survivor. For young people, the chance of death is low so it's possible to get a great deal of life insurance coverage at a modest cost.

Many couples start families and now have dependent children. Suddenly the need for life insurance coverage becomes much greater because not only do you need life insurance to replace income for your surviving spouse, but also for your children and their possible future college tuition.

If you have a house, now you need life insurance to cover your mortgage payments. During this time when your liabilities are at their peak, you will need greater insurance coverage. Fortunately as a young couple, such life insurance coverage can be affordable.

Over time, as your children graduate from college and begin their own lives, there is less need for life insurance coverage to protect your children. In addition, your mortgage liability will be much less so you'll wind up needing less insurance coverage. Of course as you age, life insurance coverage gets more expensive, but you'll need less of it.

Eventually when your mortgage is paid off, your children are no longer dependent on you, and your liabilities are much less, so you'll need less and less life insurance. At this point in your life, your retirement accounts have been fully funded and all of your short-term and long-term liabilities have been paid in full. You can now go into your golden years living off of your retirement accounts as your primary income source since you have no mortgage or debt payments. At the same time you need less life insurance, and the cost for life insurance greatly increases.

Throughout your life, you can get affordable life insurance coverage to cover your liabilities at all stages of your life. As a result, there simply is no reason not to get life insurance no matter what your income level may be to protect your family from the trauma of an untimely event, while you work towards funding your short-term and long-term financial needs.

Life insurance can be used to:

- Make provisions to take care of your family after you are dead, guaranteeing that your family will continue to receive income.

- Give your survivors choices about their future. If you own a home, your life insurance will pay off the mortgage so your family can stay in the house rather than being forced to sell it. Remember, the home is the hub of the family that will help keep the family safe and secure.

- We all want in life the best for our children, and one way to ensure that is through a great education. Life insurance will cover the college tuition so you can have peace of mind knowing that your children will be given the best chance at success in life.

- Set at least enough money aside to take care of your final expenses so your loved ones won't have to worry about funeral costs.

How much insurance you need depends on multiple factors. While some insurance providers might issue a standard response to this common question, you need coverage based on your specific needs based on income and debts.

For example, an average family might choose the coverage, or "face amount," based on five to ten times their gross income, plus their mortgage and debts. But the question is, are you average? Probably not; your coverage should factor in lifestyle, financial goals, debts and often-overlooked expenses, such as additional childcare expenses.

When determining your coverage needs, consider the following:

- The size of your family and ages of your family members
- The standard of living you'll want them to be able to maintain
- The costs for childcare or care for an elderly parent, if you are an in-home caregiver
- Future expenses such as educational, health or mortgage costs
- Final expenses likely incurred at the time of your death, including taxes, legal fees and funeral costs

Like too many people, I used to think that life insurance was only a luxury that only a few people actually needed. It wasn't until I had already started my own company with my partner that we looked at each other over lunch and realized, "What would happen if one of us should die?"

At this time, my partner and I each had about $20 million worth of shares in our company, and if one of us had died, the other person would have to buy out the remaining shares to continue running the company. Neither of us had $20 million in the bank account, and that made us realize the legal and financial mess that could have occurred.

Not only did we suddenly realize how vulnerable our entire company was in the event of one of our deaths, but we both realized that our families were completely unprotected financially. My wife was a stay-at-home mom, taking care of our two-year-old daughter. Who was going to pay the mortgage for the next twenty to thirty years? Who was going to pay for my daughter's college tuition when she got older? How could my wife possibly replace my sizeable income overnight after my death?

With our business and personal life completely naked and exposed, we had to contact a life insurance agent right away. Buying life insurance isn't like buying a shirt, but more like a puzzle where everyone's situation is different based on their needs and desires. With the help of a life insurance agent, my partner and I were able to buy the coverage we needed to protect our company and our families for a reasonable cost.

Like too many people, I used to think that life insurance was only a luxury that only a few people actually needed. It wasn't until I had already started my own company with my partner that we looked at each other over lunch and realized, "What would happen if one of us should die?"

Not only did we suddenly realize how vulnerable our entire company was in the event of one of our deaths, but we both realized that our families were completely unprotected financially. My wife was a stay-at-home mom, taking care of our one-year-old daughter. Who was going to pay the mortgage for the next twenty to thirty years? Who was going to pay for my daughter's college tuition when she got older? How could my wife possibly replace my sizeable income overnight after my death?

Types of life insurance

Now that you understand what you must consider to have adequate coverage for your family, it is equally important to understand the two basic types of life insurance: Term Insurance and Permanent Insurance. Term insurance is purely life insurance while permanent (also called "cash value" or "whole life") policies include a savings element.

Term insurance is what I like to call, "simple insurance." Term policies typically offer 10-, 20-, or 30-year policies. The term of the policy represents the amount of time the insurance policy will cover you in the event of death. For example, if you had a 20-year term life insurance policy that you purchased at the age of 35, the insurance will last until age 55. Once the term policy reaches its limit, you have the option of renewing the policy for another term if you wish.

Term life insurance policies are simple to understand because of several factors:

- It's straightforward. If you die during the term of your policy, your beneficiaries get paid the value of the term policy, such as $500,000.

- It's inexpensive. When you're young, premiums for term insurance are extremely low for the protection it provides. You aren't paying anything extra to fund a savings account or cover investment fees.

- You pay only for what you need when you need it. You typically need life insurance coverage for a specific period of time, such as while your children are living with you.

Permanent or whole-life policies combine life coverage with an investment fund. Not only are you buying a policy that pays a fixed amount on your death, but part of your premium goes toward building cash value from investments made by the insurance company.

Cash value builds tax-deferred each year that you keep the policy, and you can borrow against the cash accumulation fund without being taxed. The amount you pay usually doesn't change throughout the life of the policy.

Universal life is a type of permanent insurance policy that combines term insurance with a money market-type investment that pays a market rate of return. To get a higher return, these policies generally don't guarantee a certain rate.

Variable life and variable universal life are permanent policies with an investment fund tied to a stock or bond mutual-fund investment.

Returns are not guaranteed.

Some of the advantages of permanent life insurance include:

- Flexibility. A permanent plan can give you access to some or all of the premiums that you have been paying for in a way favorable to your taxes.

- It's with you until you die. This type of policy coverage is guaranteed for your life with no out-of-the-blue payment increases. A term policy will expire at a certain date, and a renewed policy could have much higher premiums.

- Inheritance. Maybe the best reason for a permanent policy is to make sure your estate and investments don't get taxed by the government. A permanent policy can provide peace of mind that your family and loved ones will be taken care of for the future.

Remember, the decision to buy a permanent or a term life insurance policy will depend on your situation, your age, your financial status, and other factors. If you are a young family with some investments to protect but are not financially stable, a term life policy might be best to protect those investments and your family. However, if you are financially stable with considerable investments, you might be better off purchasing a permanent plan. There is no one type of policy that is best for everyone, so you'll need the help of a qualified insurance agent to help you decide what you need and why.

Life events such as the untimely passing of you or someone you love are inevitable. The only thing you can control is the damage it will have on the family and the household balance sheet. Preparing for death is the number one inevitable life event that you must protect against.

Unfortunately, most financial advice focuses almost exclusively on paying down debt and increasing savings and income. If you focus solely on these two points and an untimely death occurs, all your efforts in reducing debt or increasing income won't help your family one bit when it's time to pay the mortgage next month or fund your children's college education ten years from now.

Being debt free when you die is not going to help your family pay their bills and maintain their lifestyle for very long. I have personally witnessed the devastating effect an unprepared family may go through when they do not have adequate life event protection. Heed my warning and do not put this off any longer. Your family deserves your attention on this matter.

My friend was living the fairytale life, beautiful wife, 2 kids, gorgeous house, luxury cars and making over $250,000 per year. I got a call from him one day to meet for coffee. He proceeded to tell me that he was diagnosed with Stage 4 lung cancer after going to the doctor to look into a cough that had been nagging him for a couple of weeks. He was 40 years old, never smoked a day in his life, and he was physically fit due to the many years that we had surfed together.

I asked him what the doctor said his survival rate was, and he told me 10%. After hearing that and trying not to break down for the first 5 minutes, I first said to him, "I am not here to steal your hopes of beating this, but I am here to help you hope for the best, but prepare for the worst."

What do you think my first question was? You guessed it, "Do you have life insurance?"

To my horror, he said no!

He not only lost his battle with cancer a few weeks later, but his wife lost the home. The children moved in with the grandparents for almost a year while the wife tried to put her life back together so she could support herself and her children under one roof again.

Heed my warning and do not put this off any longer. Your family deserves your attention to this matter because the only collateral damage your family should be dealing with when you pass is grief and grief alone.

More people understand that they need auto insurance to protect their car, yet they completely ignore the need for life insurance to protect their families. You're going to die; plan for it now while you have time. An effective financial plan is one that's well protected. Protecting your assets is actually more important than accruing more assets because no matter how much money you have, you can lose it all if you're not protected. All that you have in your life is all that you have in the world, so protect it.

When my friend first started in the mortgage industry, he got a call from a lady whose husband had just died, and she needed to take a loan out on her home just to pay her bills. Unfortunately, she didn't have a job so she had no source of income, making it impossible to get any type of loan. This woman started crying and told him, "Please try. I don't have any money and I don't know what else to do."

Her only option was to get some sort of job to earn income so she could qualify for a loan. That's when she told him, "I'm sixty years old. I don't want to lose my house. What can I do?"

When you hear stories of total strangers breaking down in tears over the phone and there's absolutely nothing you can do, you realize how wide open and vulnerable people can be at any age. That's why I wrote this book and this section in particular—because I don't want you to ever be in an unfortunate situation where you're suffering emotionally and financially just because you didn't know of a simple solution like life insurance.

Take the time now to understand the different types of life insurance policies available and do your own research. Death is inevitable but it doesn't have to be morbid because you're doing it out of care to protect your loved ones.

In this chapter, you learned:

- Getting good life insurance is one of the best decisions you can make for your family in the event of your death.
- Many financial difficulties can occur if one spouse dies. If you're married or have children, you need to plan for their futures as well as your own.
- There are several different kinds of life insurance, including term and permanent.

XIV. Set Aside Emergency Cash and Food

In this chapter, you will learn about emergency cash and food, and you will put in place your own emergency cash account and build a basic food reserve.

Before you take up your notebook and get online or into the library, here are just a few observations about establishing an emergency fund to get you thinking.

Life is an exercise in the unexpected; things happen! You need a little bit of a cushion, a buffer to help you get through unexpected events. The furnace or water heater give out. The garage door spring breaks. You get laid off for a little while. A child is invited to a tournament or competition requiring air travel. Into your budget you need to plan to set aside a little cash and to build a one-month food storage reserve of water, food, medicine, sanitation, clothing, and shelter.

Put aside some cash in an emergency fund

An emergency savings fund is one of the fundamental building blocks in your family's financial foundation. You need an emergency savings fund even before you start paying off high-interest debt because you must plan for unforeseen emergencies that won't be covered by life, health, or disability insurance.

An emergency fund is strictly for dire financial emergencies. You should never withdraw money from your emergency fund to buy luxury items. If you want something such as a vacation or a new car, you should plan for it by creating a separate savings account.

While you may have an investment account or a retirement account that you could use in an emergency, you may not want to withdraw funds from these accounts for a number of reasons including bad market timing, early withdrawal penalties, or a delay in the liquidity of actually selling your investment and receiving your funds. An investment account is meant to grow over time, and a retirement account should only be used for money after you retire. Withdrawing funds from these accounts prematurely will simply side-track your goals.

An emergency savings fund is a separate account that should only be used for emergencies and nothing else. You don't use it to save up for a new TV, remodel the house, or go on vacation. An emergency savings fund is meant to provide a financial cushion to pay for unexpected bills such as:

- Lost job due to layoff
- Reduced income due to less working hours
- Repair bills for fixing cars, homes, or appliances
- Replacement costs due to theft or damage
- Pet health care
- Unexpected taxes owed to IRS

Death in family that required you to help pay for funeral and other expenses

Unexpected medical expenses not fully covered by insurance

While there are numerous emergencies that can occur at any time, most emergencies are minor in nature. For example, paying money for a veterinarian to help a sick or injured pet may be unexpected, but it's not likely to cause long-term damage to your family's finances. Likewise if your car needs new brakes, the cost may be more than you might want to pay, but you can often pay such bills on credit without causing undue hardship.

How much is enough? As usual, the exact amount depends on your circumstances (your income and your needs) to decide how much you should save.

To calculate how much money your emergency savings account should hold, let's take a look at a fictional John Smith who earns $50,000 a year, taking home a net income of $32,000 after taxes.

John Smith should have an emergency savings fund containing at least $32,000 (the same amount as his net income after taxes). While this may seem like a lot of money, you can save this amount over a period of time, such as ten years. That means John Smith simply needs to save $3,200 a year for ten years, or $266.67 a month for ten years.

By breaking down your emergency savings amount into monthly payments, you can simply treat this as another cost center to pay every month like insurance. Building up your emergency savings fund won't happen overnight, but planning for job loss is a necessity in life and therefore you must start contributing to the account today. Once you've reached your emergency savings fund goal, then you can stop saving and allocate that money somewhere else.

To give you a place to start as you engage with your notebook in your prototype thinking, consider this list of things you might do to establish an emergency fund. Remember to take good notes on what you learn, what you observe about what people are saying, and what you think makes sense for you.

Keep good notes.

"21 Strategies for Creating an Emergency Fund, and Why It's Critical"
Post written by Leo Babauta, July 31, 2007
http://zenhabits.net/21-strategies-for-creating-an-emergency-fund-and-why-its-critical/

1. *Start small. If you don't have much to save, it doesn't matter—the important thing is just to start. Even if it's only $25 per paycheck, just start. It will slowly grow each paycheck, and you will be glad to see at least a little in your savings, and will soon be motivated to try to save more.*

2. *Automatic deduction. This is common advice, but that's because it works. Set up an online savings account (such as ING Direct or Emigrant Direct) and have it automatically deduct an amount each payday. If you don't have to think about it, saving will be much easier.*

3. *Payroll deduction. If you have discipline problems, there are accounts where you can have the amount deducted directly from your paycheck, before it's deposited into your checking account (or before your employer cuts the paycheck).*

4. *Treat it as a bill. Every payday, you have a list of bills to pay before you can spend any of your money on variable expenses such as gas, groceries or eating out. Well, add your emergency fund contribution to your list of bills, and pay it at the same time. This makes it non-negotiable, and then what's left over is what you can spend on other stuff.*

5. *Reduce an expense, save it. Take a look at how you're spending money now, and find some things that can be cut back. Magazine purchases, gourmet coffee, comic books, cable TV, gizmos and gadgets. Whatever you decide to cut back on, take that same amount and put it directly into savings each paycheck. Don't spend it.*

6. *Round up. I got this tip from J.D. Roth of Get Rich Slowly ... actually, it's a strategy used by his wife, who will log every purchase or check she writes into her checkbook or finance software—but rounds up to the nearest dollar. So if she spends $26.01, she enters it as $27. Over the course of a month, this can add up to decent savings.*

7. *Double purpose account. This tip is from Trent of The Simple Dollar, who wanted to pay down his debts but still have the financial security of an emergency fund at the same time. So Trent brilliantly used a double-purpose account: he would save money in an account, and after he reached a certain minimum, anything above that amount was being saved to pay off a specific debt. So let's say the minimum amount is $500. After you pass $500, the money being saved is for a $200 debt (for example). Once you reach $700 in your savings account, you can pay off the $200 debt completely. Repeat the process for each debt.*

8. *Tip yourself. If you go to a restaurant and tip a waiter 15 or 20 percent, for example, match that tip for yourself. So if your tip is $10, tip yourself $10 as well ... and put that directly in savings.*

9. *Keep paying debt, but to yourself. If you finish making a car payment, or paying off a credit card or smaller debt, take the amount you were paying to that debt and put it directly in savings each month. You won't feel a difference in your budget.*

10. *Budget big for groceries, then save the difference. Let's say you normally spend between $320 and $375 on groceries. Budget $400 for groceries, and whatever you don't spend of that $400, put it in savings.*

11. *Quit smoking or drinking. Well, I wouldn't bet my emergency fund on quitting one of these two addictions, but if you do quit, you should take the amount you were spending (ad that's a considerable amount, I know) and put it into savings. For me, I spent more than $5 a day on smoking—and when I quit in November 2005, it freed up $150 a month for savings.*

12. *Limit your access. If you are tempted to spend your savings, you should put it in an account that is hard to get to. Put your savings in a money market account or fund, and when it reaches a certain amount, roll it over into a CD or Treasury bond. You might not make as much on a CD, for example, but the point is that it's hard to access and requires less discipline.*

13. *Stash a bonus or tax refund. If you get a Christmas bonus, or a tax refund, or some other such windfall, put that directly in the bankand don't spend it. Use it for your emergency fund. Now start paying off your debt.*

14. *Save your change. Don't spend any coins you get. When you get home at the end of the day, empty out your pockets into a jar, and once a month, go to the bank and put it into savings. This can add up faster than you think.*

15. *Save dollar bills. Similar to the above strategy, get your cash in $20 bills, or $10s or $5s. Don't carry $1 bills. When you get $1 bills as change, don't spend them. When you get home, put those $1 bills in an envelope, and save them.*

16. *Refinance. Refinancing your mortgage or auto loan can save you a lot of money. Take the amount you save and put it in savings.*

17. *Sell your car. If you have two cars, see if you can live without one of them. That's what my wife and I do, and it works out fine, even with six kids. Take the amount you were paying on the second car and save it. Or, alternatively, sell your car and buy a cheaper used model. Save the difference in the payments.*

18. *Cut out dessert. If you're trying to lose weight, don't order the dessert or junk food you would normally order. Instead, put the amount you would have spent in an envelope and save it.*

19. *Stay in. Instead of going to the movies or eating out, cook your own meals and watch a DVD—or do something fun for free. Save the difference.*

XIV. Set Aside Emergency Cash and Food

20. *Freelance. Take your skills and market them as a freelancer, or get a second job on the side. Take the extra income and bank it. This was one of my strategies, and it works great.*

21. *Save on auto insurance. If you can switch to liability insurance, you might be able to save hundreds of dollars. Take the extra amount you would have paid for insurance and save it.*

That's a great list of things one could do to get the money to put a little each month into an emergency fund.

Establish a simple reserve of food

As with an emergency cash fund, you should slowly build up a reserve of water, food, medicine, sanitation, clothing, and shelter. Look at what it would take you and your family to survive a natural disaster or a work-related event such as an accident or loss of job that would severely limit your ability to go to the store to buy supplies.

Many people and organizations have literature and videos and seminars on food storage and emergency preparedness, so take the time now to ask about these resources at your local city offices, your church, or your library. Free literature on how much to store, how to store it, how to make sure you rotate it so it does not spoil and waste, etc. are all available. Does your city or community have an emergency plan that you can count on in a natural disaster? Find out about it.

Keep the whole project simple and intuitive; store only those things that are essential and that you and yours actually use. Just enough to sustain you for 30 days.

Learn also how to prepare the foods that you store, with menus and trial baking events where you prepare the recipes and eat the food. Consider sanitation and handling bodily waste if the water and electricity are out.

To get a good list of things to be concerned about and items to store, go to an emergency preparedness business in your community and walk through the aisles, thinking about what you see and what you might need.

Your prototyping notebook will serve you well as you investigate this subject of food and emergency supplies and equipment. It will help you focus on the few things that will really make a difference rather than on all of the really neat and interesting and clever things and ideas available in this market. Many people waste a lot of money and time on things that are impractical.

In this chapter, you learned:

- Things happen. Be prepared as best you can by putting aside some emergency cash.
- Consider your emergency fund non-negotiable. Take a set amount of money and put that into savings each and every month.
- Planning for the future extends beyond money.
- You may want to have a supply of food.

credit card number

postal address

birthdate

bank account numbers

social security number

name

email address

company

bank information

telephone number

XV. Provide Identity Theft Protection

What is identity theft?

Identity theft occurs when someone uses your personally identifying information, like your name, Social Security number, or credit card number, without your permission, to commit fraud or other crimes. The FTC estimates that as many as 9 million Americans have their identities stolen each year. In fact, you or someone you know may have experienced some form of identity theft. The crime takes many forms. Identity thieves may rent an apartment, obtain a credit card, or establish a telephone account in your name. You may not find out about the theft until you review your credit report or a credit card statement and notice charges you didn't make—or until you're contacted by a debt collector. Identity theft is serious. While some identity theft victims can resolve their problems quickly, others spend hundreds of dollars and many days repairing damage to their good name and credit record. Some consumers victimized by identity theft may lose out on job opportunities, or be denied loans for education, housing or cars because of negative information on their credit reports. In rare cases, they may even be arrested for crimes they did not commit."

(Deter, Detect, Defend - Fighting Back Against Identity Theft, Federal Trade Commission, http://www.ftc.gov/bcp/edu/microsites/idtheft/consumers/about-identity-theft.html)

In this chapter, you will learn about identity theft protection, and you will put in place your own identify theft protection program.

My purpose in this book is to help you prosper and find financial security. Budgets, wills and trusts, home-based business and taxes, insurance, emergency money and food—all of these tools have been put in place now to help you keep your money and to safeguard your wealth. Another threat, like disability or death, that could be a catastrophic threat to your financial well being is a risk that is peculiar to the technologies of this day in which we live: identity theft.

We live today in a very dangerous digital and interconnected world. We protect ourselves and our children from physical crimes, but with digital information and cloud-based commerce, we are more vulnerable to crime against us than ever before. You must take the same precautions against information theft as you do with locking your car door or your house from theft.

The difference with information theft is that once your information is stolen and put into the information network of the underground black market, it is almost impossible to stop the trafficking of your identity, so the crime and damage continues year after year. We may not be able to fully protect ourselves from identity theft, but a good security plan can protect your information so the thieves will move on to find easier prey.

According to the U.S. Department of Justice, identity theft is the fastest-growing financial crime in the U.S. and perhaps the fastest growing crime of any kind in the country, with $49.3 billion lost to identity theft just in 2007. The Federal Trade Commission also states that over 9 million Americans fall victim to identity theft each year.

Identity theft is possibly the single biggest risk of crime exposure today where one in twenty Americans will be an identity theft victim according to a 2010 report released by the Javelin Strategy and Research Company. As a result, identity theft poses tremendous risks to a family's financial foundation. If you lock your doors and windows to keep strangers from breaking into your house and stealing your money, you need to take similar precautions to protect your money from identity theft as well.

Identity theft is a potentially catastrophic life event

Just like an untimely death, disability or job loss, identity theft has a very similar financial and emotional impact on a family's finances. Thus identity theft is fast becoming a major life event that everyone needs to protect against.

Basically identity theft works because our identities are no longer limited to paper documents and meeting people face to face. Instead, our identities are reduced to bits of information stored on an anonymous computer. If someone can steal those bits of information, they can impersonate the real person that information represents. Computers can't tell that a sixty-five-year-old woman ordering electronic equipment over the Internet is really a twenty-year-old-kid in Russia impersonating that woman over the Internet. As long as that kid has that woman's data that defines her identity, such as her Social Security number, bank account numbers, birthdate, and address, he can impersonate her by charging items to her credit card while draining her bank accounts at the same time.

Identity thieves aren't just malicious teenagers in your neighborhood but organized crime cartels around the world. It's an easy, faceless crime that doesn't involve even knowing the victim. As a result, identity theft has become a worldwide, billion dollar black market industry that can and will affect everybody. We live in a society of digital information, and that information can be stolen at any time by anyone around the world.

Identity theft cannot only devastate a family financially but emotionally as well. When identity theft victims call a law firm, they can be helped to fix the financial damage (including bankruptcy to get out from the liability of debts that identity thieves accumulated under that person's name), but the emotional impact stays with them forever.

A 2008 survey by the Identity Theft Resource Center shows that 37 percent of identity theft victims showed feelings of defilement, 60 percent felt betrayed, 21 percent felt a loss of innocence and 63 percent felt a sense of powerlessness. The long-term emotional responses showed that 30 percent felt they were unable to trust people, 4 percent felt suicidal, 25 percent were ready to "give up the fight" and 10 percent believed they had lost everything.

Identity theft victims often become restrictive in the information they share with others, even their own attorneys. They may refuse to exchange any type of information over a telephone or the Internet, preferring to only exchange any sensitive data face-to-face. They no longer trust anyone and feel as if they are trapped on a protective island all by themselves.

How thieves steal your identity

Identity theft starts with the misuse of your information that personally identifies you such as your name, Social Security number, credit card numbers, and other financial account information. For identity thieves, this information is as good as gold.

Skilled identity thieves use a variety of methods to steal your information, including:

Dumpster
Diving

1. Dumpster Diving: Rummage through trash looking for bills or other paper with your personal information on it.

Skimming

2. Skimming: Steal credit/debit card numbers by using a special device that can read the data stored on the magnetic strip. Skimmers are often placed on gas station pumps or other machines that accept credit cards, or are used by people who have access to your credit card such as a waiter or hotel clerk.

Phishing

3. Phishing: Send phony e-mail messages pretending to be from financial institutions or companies and trick you into responding by revealing your personal information.

Changing
Your Address

4. Changing Your Address: Divert your billing statements to another location by completing a change of address form at the post office.

Old-Fashioned
Stealing

5. Old-Fashioned Stealing: Steal wallets and purses; mail, including bank and credit card statements; pre-approved credit offers; and new checks or tax information. They steal personnel records, or bribe employees who have access.

Pretexting

6. Pretexting: Use false pretenses to obtain your personal information from financial institutions, telephone companies, and other sources.

The first time I heard about identity theft was in 1998. The police called a friend and stated that a rash of identity theft had taken place that they traced to his company's dumpster located in the farthest corner of the parking lot. Back in 1998, his mortgage company was just a couple of years old, and I was not aware of the threat of identity theft.

In case you're wondering why someone would target a dumpster of a mortgage company, let me describe the amount of information a loan application has on it. By the time someone completes an application for a home loan, they will know more about your personal and financial life than even your own parents. When you fill out an application to borrow hundreds of thousands of dollars, lenders want to know everything about you, including but not limited to: where you live, work, how much money you make, your bank account information from account numbers to balances, your credit score and your credit account information, your past and present residence information and any other information they deem fit to make a credit decision. The amount of information consolidated into a single loan application contains more than enough information for someone to steal that person's identity.

Before they knew the risks and the methods that thieves would go through to retrieve this type of information, they unknowingly dumped out clients' loan applications in the trash. The police explained how someone had gone dumpster diving to retrieve discarded loan application forms. Every night, they were literally throwing clients' sensitive personal data right into the hands of identity thieves.

After learning about our vulnerability to dumpster diving, they immediately made a mandatory policy to shred all client information upon completion of its use. They brought in big shredder bins and located them all throughout their facility to ensure that not a single piece of client information could escape intact from their office. By law, they had to keep all funded loan applications for a minimum of 3 years, so they secured those files in a protected file box and stored them in a locked and guarded file storage facility.

They were not bound by any laws to follow so many protective procedures, but they definitely felt it was their corporate duty to protect their clients. They not only instituted a shred and secure policy, but as they continued to grow throughout the years, they required background checks on all potential employees looking for prior theft convictions to prevent an identity thief from becoming an employee. They secured the building with electronic badges for entry and exit to log all who came and went. They installed security cameras throughout the campus inside and outside of the facilities. As technology in the early 90s began to get better, they moved their process to paperless filing as much as possible, reducing the amount of paper information that could be copied.

How you can protect your identity

"While nothing can guarantee that you won't become a victim of identity theft, you can minimize your risk, and minimize the damage if a problem develops, by making it more difficult for identity thieves to access your personal information.

Protect your Social Security number
Treat your trash and mail carefully
Be on guard when using the Internet
Select intricate passwords
Verify sources before sharing information
Safeguard your purse and wallet
Store information in secure locations."
(http://www.ftc.gov/bcp/edu/microsites/idtheft/consumers/deter.html)

As diligent and persistent as identity thieves can be, there are ways that you can protect yourself from this pervasive crime so you don't have to lose hundreds or thousands of dollars, spend hours rectifying your financials, or suffer from damaged credit scores. Even worse, some people spend years suffering the effects of identity theft without realizing it through lost job offers, being denied loans, and other lost opportunities because someone else has charged items in their name and hurt their credit history as a result.

Unfortunately, there's no single, simple way to protect yourself against identity theft. However, you can minimize your risk to identity theft by following a comprehensive plan and maintaining a paranoid mindset when it comes to guarding your personal information.

Remember, thieves are very cunning and pervasive and can circumvent every possible protective measure you put in place. All you can do is make it difficult for them and hopefully deter them to find a more visible and vulnerable victim. Here are a few tips to consider making it difficult to getting access to your personal information:

1. Shred All Identifying Documents, Bank Slips, Etc.

   Bank deposit receipts, credit card statements, old documents, anything with sensitive information should be properly disposed of. If you don't have a fireplace, consider investing in a low-cost paper shredder. Identity thieves can learn a lot from rifling through trash; don't let yours give away your identity.

2. Check Your Credit Report

   According to US law, every citizen is entitled to one free credit report each year. You can get the free report from the three major credit agencies by going to Annualcreditreport. com. Verify that the information is correct and check for suspicious activity, particularly mysterious new accounts opened. For even better protection, sign up for a service that notifies you when changes occur to your credit report.

3. Secure Your Important Documents

   Your Social Security card, passport, birth certificate and other identifying materials are highly sought-after by identity thieves and can command top dollar on the black market. Be sure that your documents are safely stored, preferably in a locked box tucked away and out of sight. Do not regularly carry these documents on you. When you travel, pay special attention to securing your passport. Leave it in a hotel room safe at all times whenever possible.

XV. Provide Identity Theft Protection

4. Be Vigilant About Your Social Security Number

Some institutions—insurers, colleges, etc.—prefer to use your social security number as their identification number for you. This is very foolish because your social security number can gain access to much of your private information. Do not allow any institution to use your Social Security number for identification purposes. Substitute another number instead.

5. Be Careful With Your Mail

Of course tampering with someone's mail is a federal offense, but that doesn't stop people from doing it. Do not to let incoming mail sit in your mailbox for a long time. If you are going to be away, have the post office hold your mail for you. When sending out sensitive mail, consider dropping it off at a secure collection box or at the post office itself.

6. Don't Fall for Phishing Scams

Phishing is a technique employed by identity thieves through email or online chat services. The thief pretends to represent a company, such as PayPal or your credit card issuer, and informs you that you need to respond with some information or click on a link. The thief may even claim to represent a charity or sweepstakes giveaway. Don't fall for it. Don't respond and don't click the link, even if it appears to be legitimate. Responsible organizations will not contact you in this way

7. Beware of Telephone Scams

Never give out personal information over the phone to someone who calls, claiming to represent a bank, credit card company, charity, or other organization. People are not always who they claim to be. You could be talking to a scam artist who is sweet-talking you out of your credit card or bank account number. This is an old scam, but still widely practiced today because it works. Don't let it work on you.

There's no end to the schemes and scams that unscrupulous people will come up with to part you from your money. Awareness, caution, good sense, and a little healthy paranoia will go a long way towards protecting you from becoming the next victim of identity theft.

Remember, you've worked hard for your money. Don't make it easy for an identity thief to steal away everything you've worked for just because you didn't know how vulnerable your personal information really can be. You may never stop identity thieves from targeting you, but you can protect yourself as much as possible and minimize the damage before it costs you money, your credit reputation, and your financial future.

In this chapter, you learned:

- Nobody expects to have their identities stolen, but it happens.
- Identity theft is the fast-growing financial crime in the United States.
- Identity thieves have multiple ways of stealing your information, from going through your garbage to phishing.
- Checking your credit score can help alert you if anyone out there is using your personal information.

XVI. Investing

"The definition of passive income is where income is generated regardless of any effort or work. Passive income investments require an initial effort to establish the income stream, and then should be self-managing from then effort, requiring no further effort on the owner of the investment. Real Estate is not a truly passive investment when tenants move out and the owner has to put forth effort to re-rent the units. Forex investing with a managed account is truly passive. Google AdSense is passive income. Stocks splits and cash dividends is a passive investment. Remember the Ronco slogan, "Set it and forget it!... If you don't have much money to invest, you have to compensate by putting in a little more time. As your time becomes more valuable, you leverage it by finding reliable people to do the work for you.... Passive/Residual Income is what every one who would like to be financially free should strive for. I think this type of income is the only true form of financial security."

(http://geniustypes.com/five_ways_to_create_passive_income_with_ little_or_no_money/).

In this chapter, you will learn about investing, and you will put into place your own investing plan. Because you have put in place a home-based business, you now need to make sure you are not just trading your time for dollars. This is why I begin with the notion of "passive investment income" or "residual" income that keeps generating income when you are not putting in time. The idea of passive income is that it works for you; you don't work for it. When you are sleeping, it earns. When you are awake, it earns. When you have lost your job, it earns. Passive income has the potential to earn money for you 24/7. Tempting, right? That's what investing can do for you. Simply by taking some of your money and investing in stocks or bonds, you can generate passive income. (Of course, stocks can also be volatile; you have the potential to lose money too, don't forget.)

Now that you have your spending plan and are sticking to it, and now that you have your protection of your money in place with wills and trusts, insurance, emergency money and food, and identity protection, it is time to put some money aside into an "investment fund" and then to place your investment. In this chapter I will tell you the basics of investing in the future.

"The way to become wealthy and financially independent is straightforward: Stay out of debt. Live on less than you make. Invest this extra money, and then reinvest most of the proceeds. In fact, retirement with several million dollars in the bank is well within the grasp of most people.

And yet most people are deeply in debt.
One cannot become wealthy when buying a new car every couple of years.
One cannot become wealthy if one is every extra dollar is spent on clothes.
One cannot become wealthy if one is spending thousands of dollars a year on electronics and expensive data packages.

When you walk into a room, the millionaire (or potential future millionaire) won't be the one with the expensive cell phone on his belt and the fancy suit. It won't be the guy in traffic with the new car. It won't be the guy living in the Mansion. The millionaire will be the guy in the old jeans. The guy in the 2-8-year-old car. The guy in the well-built but modest home.

Let your status symbol be your paid-off mortgage. Your paid-off car. Your basket of mutual funds. Your ability to write a check whenever things happen. Your ability to pay cash for a vacation. Set your sights on the right goals, and success will follow."

(The Small Investor: Investment Strategies and Wealth Building for the Small Investor, "Is Narcissism Keeping You from Becoing Wealthy?" from the book by Twenge and Campbell, The Narcissism Epidemic: Living in the Age of Entitlement, http://smallivy.wordpress.com/).

Decide how much money you would like to invest, but please, resist the urge to put every extra penny from your savings into investing. Start small so that you can get a better feel for what you're doing without having too much money on the line. Remember our old adage, "Slow and steady wins the race"? That is especially true when it comes to investing. People confuse "investing" with "gambling." Investing is not a get-rich-quick scheme. You are not putting all of your money on a company's future, certain that you are the only one that's been able to see its potential, that you know it will be the next big thing. You must think before you act. Start by doing your prototyping, going out far and wide to get as balanced a perspective on simple or basic investing as possible.

It should go without saying, and seems incredibly appropriate after the identity theft discussion of before, that you should never trust anyone with your money until you have done your homework to vet them. Do your analysis, and pay close attention to what's going on. Have a basic plan, and never put your money anywhere until you have at least three tested, proven and reliable investment options that you've discussed with your friends and associates. You will also need to rely on your intuition here. Never put your money on anything that doesn't sit right with you. Go slowly. Go prudently. Take good notes and test your theories.

The parasites and cockroaches and shysters who are happy to take your money are so many that we often wonder, cynically, who else is "out there." Scams abound. Remember the quote from above: "The way to become wealthy and financial independent is straightforward: Stay out of debt. Live on less than you make. Invest this extra money, and then reinvest most of the proceeds."

There are two things you need to know about investing: buying and selling. That's it. Not so scary, right? In a perfect world, you buy low and sell high. That means it doesn't cost you that much to purchase a share, but when you sell your shares later they're worth significantly more. It's like the weather—you can recognize patterns to forecast, but sometimes it's going to go in a completely new direction. Resist the urge to buy and sell all of the time though. As I mentioned before, investment is a long-term strategy.

If you partake in your company's retirement plan, you're almost certainly already investing; they're just doing it on your behalf. If you feel comfortable enough, take it to the next level by deciding where to put your own money. So, how do we "invest this extra money?" The answer is one you come to by being aware. You must do your own research on this and put your money where you feel comfortable. However, don't be alarmed. There are many resources available to you that can help you get started with investing your money.

I recommend you start at this website: http://money.cnn.com/ magazines/moneymag/money101/.

Stay here a while. Read as many of the topics as you find interesting and informative. Be sure to have your notebook handy to take notes, record your thoughts, and document other URLs and websites you go to as you are exploring.

Now go to http://money.msn.com/personal-finance/ and look and read around. Take good notes, compare ideas with what you read at the CNN site. What are you learning about investing?

The Wall Street Journal, Forbes, Fortune, Business Week, and other business-related magazines and website are always informative. They will help you understand investing, how to know what is going on with various investment options, and how you might begin to put a little money here or there to test the waters. Consider subscribing to them while you are still in your prototyping stage.

You also don't have to head right on down to the stock market to invest. You can also purchase savings bonds (the US Treasury offers them) or put your money into a CD with a high interest rate. The idea here is that you are essentially placing your money somewhere and letting it grow.

As you look at the type of investments also look at the time you have available to spend or tend that investment. For example, if you want to invest in the stock market and you do not want to hire a stock broker, then think about the time it will take to get yourself educated enough and buy and sell stocks. This may be one time when it's much more efficient to hire someone to do this for you. However, even if you hire someone, you still want to consider your gut on this one. If something sounds like a bad idea, then don't put your money towards it, even if the person you hired is telling you to do it. It's your money; ultimately you get to decide where it should go.

In this chapter, you learned:

- Your money can make its own money with little to no effort on your part.
- Investing is something you can do alone or with a broker.
- There are two parts to investing: buying and selling.
- Trust your gut when it comes to investing—but do your research too.
- You don't have to play the stock market to earn interest on your money. There are less risky options.

XVII. Stay Informed, Hire Help if Needed

Congratulations!

If you managed to read up until this point, you already know more about money and personal finances than 99% of ordinary people. This is the sad truth. The sad truth is that the majority of people do not even know how to balance their checkbooks. No wonder they hardly get by—they live month to month, and they are blown away even by the softest winds of financial storms.

The fact that you decided to embark on this journey with us means that you want to be among the one percent who really cares about their finances and that you want to know what you are doing. It means that you want to stand strong against the winds that blow. And you will

Enjoy working on your finances

As I've established before, keeping your finances in order means that you have to work on them regularly, preferably every day (noting your expenses and income), every week (weekly review and plan) and every month ("reality check").

In a few weeks, you will see that working on your finances is not a chore—it is pure joy. As your financial situation ameliorates, you will find delight in counting and planning. Oh no, do not be afraid: you will not become Scrooge McDuck, bathing in money and counting all day long (though bathing in money is a nice idea, so go for it, if you want to...).

You will simply learn to love your life as it is. By following the simple steps laid out in this book, you will feel that you are no longer naked to the world. You will feel at ease. You will know where you are coming from and where you are going. You will no longer depend on anyone. You will no longer have to wait for the government, the opposition, the state administration, the federal administration. You will be the master of your own life, and that is a wonderful feeling!

Learn, learn, learn...

Now, let me add a few important things to what has been said before.

In order to be able to stay on top of your game, I recommend that you learn the basics of bookkeeping. As you have a home-based business now, bookkeeping is a competency that you will need day in, day out. Of course, you do not have to know it all, or become a bookkeeper overnight—just learn the basics so that you are not lost in the woods. If you cannot do it yourself, you should hire a professional bookkeeper to do the work for you. But do yourself a favor and please learn the basics so you can keep control of the hired help, too.

Try to follow the business news regularly. State governments and the federal government adopt new regulations every week, and businesses should comply, even if they can hardly follow the speed... Sometimes it is almost impossible to take note of all new regulations, but you should at least try, because following and respecting new tax regulations, IRS communications is a must for people who want to master their finances. A good bookkeeper might do this for you, I am aware of it, but again, you should be on top of your game and know what you are doing. Remember, you are trying to take control of your financial life!

Read books, articles about the financial system in order to understand its basics. What are banks for, how business loans work, what does Wall Street do, what is the relationship between Wall Street and Main Street? The logic of capitalism is simple, and you should be aware of the fact that the financial system is at its core. People can hate financial institutions all they want, but the clear truth is that America would be nowhere—I repeat, nowhere—without them. Financial institutions allocate capital, for instance; thus they are the ones that provide the blood in the circulatory system of our economy!

Be on top of your game and read about the functioning of our economy. You will see that its logic is simple, that it favors and rewards good services and competitive businesses (of course, when you establish a home-based business, it has to offer something competitive and interesting, but I have already established that).

New habits

Try to change the things you read and watch. We Americans spend a lot of time reading and watching trash, while we could watch and read things that nurture us. So do yourself a favor, drop your daily tabloids and go for the Financial Times. Drop the National Enquirer and go for Newsweek. Instead of watching trash movies, listen to talk shows and feed your mind. In the morning, when taking the kids to school, listen to a news station instead of what you are listening to now.

At first, you will feel overwhelmed, and maybe a little bored. I acknowledge that this will require effort on your part (but everything important is based on effort!). However, in a few days or a few weeks you will begin to enjoy your newfound knowledge and competency. You will understand everything. You will have arguments. You will begin to navigate life and business much more easily than before. To sum up, you will learn that Tom Cruise' marriage has no effect on your life, but a new tax regulation can turn it upside down (your life, not Tom Cruise' marriage). If you know about it, you can be prepared for it—contrary to 99% of ordinary people!

If you make this little effort, you will gain a completely new insight about the way the world works. Do not forget that this effort does not require time; you only have to shift and change your current habits a little bit.

Find your heroes: read a lot about successful people

Where is the fun in doing all of this, you might ask. Good question, friend! Let's talk about fun.

I know that the Financial Times might be a little dry sometimes; it might be like the veggies on your plate when all you want is a big, greasy hamburger or a big chunk of chocolate. The good news is that you can have those, too, right after the veggies.

When you try to master your finances, when you try to live up to your potential, your hamburger and chocolate will be memoirs and biographies of successful and famous people: businessmen, soldiers, generals, politicians, artists and historical figures.

If you have time to go out to the library—or better, simply make time to go out to the library—look around for memoirs and biographies. Just take a look at what's on offer.

Are you attracted by ancient history? Julius Caesar might be a good choice for you. Or go for Alexander the Great, Charlemagne, Louis XIV of France. They will all have something to teach you; you just have to read their biographies to learn what that something is. You like American history? Go for a biography of Abraham Lincoln or George Washington. You like politics? Biographies of John F. Kennedy, Ronald Reagan or Bill Clinton are out there for you. The memoirs of George W. Bush just came out. If you prefer business and industry,

Henry Ford, Steve Jobs, Bill Gates, the Rothschilds, George Soros, Donald Trump a thousand other names are out there to offer you knowledge and insight.

What I am trying to tell you is that you have to find your own heroes and learn from them what you can, including successes and failures. Mankind could become so successful because new generations do not have to do everything all over again. Human knowledge is preserved, written down and safeguarded; it is out there for you. Go for it. Use it. And enjoy it. The lives of successful and famous people (not Tom Cruise, but those who really did mark human history) are really fascinating. Try to read them, and you will learn that sometimes these readings are even better (and healthier) than chocolate.

Surround yourself with success – Net worth is based on your network

Many people cannot get out of poverty because they do not know how. (This problem is solved for you, as you are about to finish this book, and now you know how to do it.) In turn, many people cannot get out of struggling because they surround themselves with people who struggle, too.

Do you know the kind of get together where everybody complains that life is hard, where everybody explains that they do not know how to get by and so on, and so on, and so on...? These kinds of discussions can literally drag you down, depress you and fill you with a feeling of hopelessness and dread. Yuck.

Now, this is something you will have to change and something you can change. You will need to stay away from discussions like this. Granted, you cannot change your friends overnight, and this is not what I am trying to tell you. But you will have to try to surround yourself with success instead of failure.

How? Reading biographies and memoirs of successful people, this simple exercise I talked about just a minute ago, is the first step towards this goal. Secondly, look out for successful and/or ambitious people who are full of energy and who have a will to succeed. Find fellow entrepreneurs who want to achieve something. Invite them for a coffee. In 99% of cases, people say yes to such an invitation. Go out to political rallies just to meet optimistic people and ambitious politicians. Go to networking events just to meet people who are like you.

In short, begin to surround yourself with success. Begin to surround yourself with people who are the way you, yourself, want to be. You will see that they will pull you upwards. Let them do it.

Networking: another substitute for chocolate

Networking is not only about surrounding yourself with success. It is also about creating meaningful relationships with other people whom you can rely on, who can help you and whom you can help in the future.

Networking is another substitute for chocolate. It fills you with joy, happiness and optimism. In order to become a master networker, be genuinely interested in people and try not to think about networking as a business transaction or a bargain. Granted, many times these events are about swapping information and business contacts. And that's great, too. But you just try to think about these events as possibilities to meet fellow entrepreneurs, fellow optimists, who want to master their lives and their finances. This is your way to enjoy these meetings, and every business card, every new piece of information will be the icing on your networking cake.

One more thing—networking is a great opportunity to meet or to hear about good service professionals. You need a good bookkeeper? Ask those fellow entrepreneurs who come to these events. You need a good lawyer or a good financial consultant? Again, ask around. If you collect business cards, do it strategically. Hear what people say; word of mouth is the best publicity out there. If a professional is talked about, they must be good.

There are many business communities out there that organize regular networking events, and there are even business communities that are 100% about networking and swapping contacts and information. Find them. Use them. And most importantly, enjoy yourself.

Hire help if needed

You might think that I want you to become a straight A MBA student overnight. That is not the case, and that is not required of you in order to be able to master your finances. Yes, learn the basics of bookkeeping, and yes, follow the news. Learn about the new regulations and bills adopted by state legislatures and the federal government. Yes, learn about the financial system and about business as much as you can.

But do not sweat it. If you are stuck or feel overwhelmed, hire help. Hire a bookkeeper, a financial consultant and a lawyer who can address your problems professionally. But you will see that you will feel more at ease with them if you know what you want and what they are talking about.

Help yourself, and Heaven will help you too. It is as simple as that.

In this chapter, you learned:

- You must continue to work on your finances if you want them to get better.

- Learning the basics of bookkeeping can take your finances to the next level.

- Follow the business news to stay abreast of what's happening and how it affects you.

- You can learn a lot from those who have gone before you. Snatch up memoirs and biographies from your financial mentors and absorb them.

- It's always possible to hire someone to help you with this stuff. It's better than not dealing with it at all.

XVIII. Conclusion or Challenge

"The only thing that's going to get you out of a financial mess is to stop doing the 'bad' and start doing the 'good':

'Stop' spending money you don't have and 'start' living within your means.

'Stop' flying by the seat of your pants and 'start' making a plan for how you're going to change things.

'Stop' making excuses and 'start' making changes.

'Stop' whining and 'start' taking responsibility for your past mistakes."

(Vax-Oxlade, Debt-Free Forever: Take Control of Your Money and Your Life, 5).

So, cause and effect/actions and consequences! The Law of Life!

What positive actions are you going to take now, so you will reap the positive results later? It follows as the light of morning does the dark of night; if you put in place the positive "causes" of prosperity and financial security, you will realize the positive "effects" of that preparation. It is the law of life. Make it work for you as you seek to build a solid foundation for prosperity and financial security in your life.

The following list is a checklist of the things you have done:

I DID IT	DATE ACCOMPLISHED	NOTES
Attitude/Commitment/ Momentum		
Analyze your Situation		
Budget and Home-Based Business		
Will and Trust		
Life Insurance		
Emergency Cash and Food		
Identity Theft		
Investment		

Exercise your will to choose a positive attitude and make a strong commitment. Then shove off to start to building the momentum of your financial security project.

Establish a spending plan and set-up a home-based business to control your taxes.

Prepare your will and set up a family trust.

Get sufficient life insurance.

Set aside emergency money and emergency food.

Proof yourself against identity theft.

Put in place an investment plan and put money in an investment.

I am proud of you for all of the steps you have taken so far. You now have everything you need to move toward prosperity and financial security. It is up to you to take this advice and move forward. Don't forget, you can do this. It's about progress, not perfection. Every little bit gets you closer to your end goal. So what are you waiting for?

To The Top!

XIX. About the Author

Eric Tippetts is a speaker, author, and coach with 19 years in the Customer Relationship Management (CRM) industry, Eric is an expert in creating and keeping relationships. As President of The Expense Tracker, Eric oversees all Sales of this powerful program that helps entrepreneurs quickly become profitable and can be seen across the country and internationally speaking at live events.

Eric's programs were recently named "#1 'must have' financial programs in the Direct Sales Industry" by a top trade magazine. These same programs are utilized by over 150,000 individuals and Eric has trained tens of thousands at live events on "how to become profitable within 7 days" of starting your own small business.

Eric's experience with many top companies like 3M, Proctor & Gamble, The Boeing Company, Mona Vie, Mannatech, Melaleuca, Nuskin and many more, has caused several publications to quote him in articles published in several top magazines including USA Today, LA Times, NY Times, Forbes, Redbook, Elle, Selling Power Magazine, and many more.

He has also appeared on numerous TV Shows including Good Things Utah, Fox Business News, ESPN, ABC, NBC, CBS, and many more.

Eric lives in Southern California, USA with his wife and daughter.

XX. Resources

Tools/Resources

- www.erictippetts.com

Website

- http://money.msn.com/personal-finance/
- http://money.cnn.com/magazines/moneymag/money101/
- http://www.socialsecurity.gov/estimator/
- http://cgi.money.cnn.com/tools/retirementplanner/retirement-planner.jsp
- http://www.bankrate.com/calculators/savings/simple-savings-calculator.aspx
- http://cgi.money.cnn.com/tools/networth/networth.html

- http://www.bankrate.com/calculators/smart-spending/personal-net-worth-calculator.aspx

Publications

- Financial Times
- The Wall Street Journal
- Business Week
- Fortune
- Forbes